D0503756

INSIDE

LANGUAGE • LITERACY • CONTENT

NATIONAL GEOGRAPHIC LEARNING | CENGAGE Learning

Acknowledgments
Grateful acknowledgment is given to the authors, artists, photographers, museums, publishers, and agents for permission to reprint copyrighted material. Every effort has been made to secure the appropriate permission. If any omissions have been made or if corrections are required, please contact the Publisher.

Photographic Credits
Cover (front): Leafcutter Bee on Fishhook Barrel Cactus Blossom, Sonoran Desert, Arizona, USA, John Cancalosi. Photograph © John Cancalosi/Peter Arnold/Getty Images.

Acknowledgments continue on page 191.

Copyright © 2014 National Geographic Learning, Cengage Learning

ALL RIGHTS RESERVED. No part of this work covered by the copyright herein may be reproduced, transmitted, stored, or used in any form or by any means graphic, electronic, or mechanical, including but not limited to photocopying, recording, scanning, digitizing, taping, web distribution, information networks, or information storage and retrieval systems, except as permitted under Section 107 or 108 of the 1976 United States Copyright Act, without the prior written permission of the publisher.

National Geographic and the Yellow Border are registered trademarks of the National Geographic Society.

For product information and technology asistance, contact us at
Cengage Learning Customer & Sales Support, 1-800-354-9706

For permission to use material from this text or product, submit all requests online at **www.cengage.com/permissions**
Further permissions questions can be emailed to
permissionrequest@cengage.com

National Geographic Learning | Cengage Learning
1 Lower Ragsdale Drive
Building 1, Suite 200
Monterey, CA 93940

Cengage Learning is a leading provider of customized learning solutions with office locations around the globe, including Singapore, the United Kingdom, Australia, Mexico, Brazil, and Japan. Locate your local office at **www.cengage.com/global**.

Visit National Geographic Learning online at **ngl.cengage.com**
Visit our corporate website at **www.cengage.com**

ISBN: 978-12857-34712 (Practice Book)
ISBN: 978-12857-34668 (Practice Book Teacher's Annotated Edition)

ISBN: 978-12857-67963 (Practice Masters)
Teachers are authorized to reproduce the practice masters in this book in limited quantity and solely for use in their own classrooms.

Printed in the United States of America
Print Number: 17 Print Year: 2024

INSIDE

LANGUAGE • LITERACY • CONTENT

NATIONAL GEOGRAPHIC LEARNING | CENGAGE Learning®

Contents

Foundations of Reading

Letters and Sounds: *Ss, Mm, Ff, Hh, Tt, Aa* F2
High Frequency Words: *am, I, is, school, the, this* F4
High Frequency Words: *a, an, here, my, no, you* F5
High Frequency Words: *at, it, look, of, on, yes* F6
Blend Words with Short *a* F7
Letters and Sounds: *Nn, Ll, Pp, Gg, Ii* F10
High Frequency Words: *are, good, see, show, where, he* F12
High Frequency Words: *answer, she, some, time, who, your* F13
High Frequency Words: *point, read, to, with, work, write* F14
Blend Words with Short *i* F15
Letters and Sounds: *Rr, Dd, Cc, Vv, Oo* F18
High Frequency Words: *do, does, for, help, in, like* F20
High Frequency Words: *around, me, picture, will, and, don't* F21
High Frequency Words: *food, not, that, both, get, these* F22
Blend Words with Short *o* F23
Letters and Sounds: *Jj, Bb, Ww, Kk, Ee* F26
High Frequency Words: *things, little, old, them, those, very* F28
High Frequency Words: *think, take, give, which, can, play* F29
High Frequency Words: *too, feel, has, have, how, put* F30
Blend Words with Short *e* F31
Letters and Sounds: *Zz, Yy, Uu, Qq, Xx* F34
High Frequency Words: *they, great, later, soon, tomorrow, call* F36
High Frequency Words: *name, need, number, we, what, book* F37
High Frequency Words: *boy, day, girl, group, letters, night, year* F38
Blend Words with Short *u* F39

Unit 1

Unit Launch **Mind Map:** Personal Information 1

▶ **Language Development**
Grammar: Pronouns 2
Grammar: Present Tense Verbs: *Am, Is,* and *Are* 4
Vocabulary: Communication. 5
Comprehension: Identify Sequence 6

▶ **Language and Literacy**
High Frequency Words: *from, home, new, go, there* 7
High Frequency Words: *many, first, next, then, one* 8
Phonics and Decoding: Short *a* and Short *o* 9
Build Reading Fluency: Expression. 13
Written Conventions: Statements and Exclamations 14

▶ **Language and Content**
Key Vocabulary: "Many People to Meet" 15

▶ **Writing Project**
Plan and Write: E-mail 17
Check Your Work 18

Unit 2

Unit Launch **Mind Map:** Foods. 19

▶ **Language Development**
Vocabulary: Colors, Shapes, and Sizes 20
Vocabulary: Foods 21
Grammar: Action Verbs 22
Comprehension: Identify Steps in a Process. 23

Unit 2, continued

▶ **Language and Literacy**
High Frequency Words: *something, make, long, large, move* 24
High Frequency Words: *different, small, open, same, eat* 25
Phonics and Decoding: Short *i* and Short *u* 26
Build Reading Fluency: Phrasing 30
Grammar: Negative Sentences 31

▶ **Language and Content**
Key Vocabulary: "U.S. Tour of Food Groups" 32

▶ **Writing Project**
Plan and Write: How-To Card 34
Check Your Work 35

Unit 3

Unit Launch **Mind Map:** Workers, Jobs, and Tools 36

▶ **Language Development**
Vocabulary: Actions and Careers 37
Grammar: Present Tense Verbs 38
Vocabulary: Tools and Careers 39
Comprehension: Identify Details 40

▶ **Language and Literacy**
High Frequency Words: *study, learn, carry, find, use* 41
High Frequency Words: *love, face, when, want, say* 42
Phonics and Decoding: Short *e* 43
Phonics and Decoding: Final *ll, ss, zz, ck* 45
Phonics and Decoding: Words with *sh* 46
Build Reading Fluency: Intonation 47
Grammar: Questions with *Who, What, Where,* and *When* 48

▶ **Language and Content**
Key Vocabulary: "Geologists — Rock Scientists" 49

▶ **Writing Project**
Plan and Write: Interview a Worker 51
Check Your Work 52

Unit 4

Unit Launch **Mind Map:** Numbers Tell Us 53

▶ **Language Development**
Grammar: Questions with *Do* and *Does* 54
Vocabulary: Cardinal Numbers 55
Grammar: Negative Sentences 56
Vocabulary: Ordinal Numbers 57
Comprehension: Identify Problem and Solution 58

▶ **Language and Literacy**
High Frequency Words: *leave, two, out, three, all* 59
High Frequency Words: *says, second, without, enough, more* 60
Phonics and Decoding: Words with Digraphs 61
Phonics and Decoding: Words with Blends and Digraphs 62
Phonics and Decoding: Words with Blends 63
Build Reading Fluency: Phrasing 64
Written Conventions: Contractions with *not* 65

▶ **Language and Content**
Key Vocabulary: "The Mighty Maya" 66

▶ **Writing Project**
Plan and Write: Research a Country 68
Check Your Work 69

Unit 5

Unit Launch **Mind Map:** How to Find Out About Your City 70

▶ **Language Development**

Vocabulary: Location Words 71
Vocabulary: Neighborhood 72
Grammar: Regular Past Tense Verbs 73
Comprehension: Identify Details 75

▶ **Language and Literacy**

High Frequency Words: *city, above, by, sometimes, her* 76
High Frequency Words: *come, animals, people, down, under* 77
Phonics and Decoding: Words with Long and Short Vowels 78
Phonics and Decoding: Multisyllabic Words 80
Build Reading Fluency: Expression 82
Written Conventions: Pronoun-Verb Contractions 83

▶ **Language and Content**

Key Vocabulary: "San Francisco" 84

▶ **Writing Project**

Plan and Write: Journal Page 86
Check Your Work 87

Unit 6

Unit Launch **Mind Map:** Family Life 88

▶ **Language Development**

Vocabulary: Family 89
Grammar: Present Tense Verbs: *Have* and *Has* 90
Vocabulary: Household Objects 91
Comprehension: Identify Details that Support a Main Idea 92

▶ **Language and Literacy**

High Frequency Words: *family, together, other, really, father* 93
High Frequency Words: *mother, our, watch, eyes, head* 94
Phonics and Decoding: Words with Long Vowels 95
Phonics and Decoding: Words with Short and Long Vowels 97
Phonics and Decoding: Plurals 98
Build Reading Fluency: Phrasing 99
Grammar: Plural Nouns 100

▶ **Language and Content**

Key Vocabulary: "The Family Reunion" 101

▶ **Writing Project**

Plan and Write: Descriptions 103
Check Your Work 104

Unit 7

Unit Launch **Mind Map:** Pack Your Bags—For the Rain Forest! 105

▶ **Language Development**

Grammar: Commands 106
Vocabulary: Landforms and Transportation 107
Vocabulary: Weather and Clothing 108
Grammar: Use the Verb *Can* 109
Comprehension: Classify Information 110

Unit 7, continued

▶ **Language and Literacy**

High Frequency Words: *places, important, world, always, or* . . . 111
High Frequency Words: *river, through, once, water, below* . . . 112
Phonics and Decoding: Words with Long *a* . . . 113
Phonics and Decoding: Words with Long *a*, Long *e*, and Long *o* . . . 114
Phonics and Decoding: Words with Short and Long Vowels . . . 115
Phonics and Decoding: Multisyllabic Words . . . 116
Build Reading Fluency: Phrasing . . . 117
Written Conventions: Capitalization—Proper Nouns . . . 118

▶ **Language and Content**

Key Vocabulary: "The Water Planet" . . . 119

▶ **Writing Project**

Plan and Write: Travel Guide . . . 121
Check Your Work . . . 122

Unit 8

Unit Launch **Mind Map:** Friends . . . 123

▶ **Language Development**

Grammar: Past Tense Verbs . . . 124
Vocabulary: Feelings . . . 125
Grammar: Irregular Past Tense Verbs: *Was* and *Were* . . . 126
Grammar: Negative Sentences and Contractions with *Not* . . . 127
Comprehension: Identify Causes and Effects . . . 128

▶ **Language and Literacy**

High Frequency Words: *saw, was, were, their, said* . . . 129
High Frequency Words: *began, about, dance, thought, again* . . . 130
Phonics and Decoding: Verbs with *-ed*. . . . 131
Build Reading Fluency: Phrasing . . . 133
Written Conventions: Possessive Nouns . . . 134

▶ **Language and Content**

Key Vocabulary: "Hand in Hand" . . . 135

▶ **Writing Project**

Plan and Write: Memory Story . . . 137
Check Your Work . . . 138

Unit 9

Unit Launch **Mind Map:** Celebrations . . . 139

▶ **Language Development**

Grammar: Adverbs . . . 140
Grammar: Present Progressive Verbs . . . 141
Vocabulary: Country Words . . . 142
Grammar: Phrases with *Like To* and *Want To*. . . . 143
Comprehension: Classify Information . . . 144

▶ **Language and Literacy**

High Frequency Words: *celebrate, most, young, children, started* . . . 145
High Frequency Words: *beginning, change, another, only, following* . . . 146
Phonics and Decoding: Verbs with *-ing* . . . 147
Build Reading Fluency: Intonation . . . 148

▶ **Language and Content**

Key Vocabulary: "Kite Festival" . . . 149

▶ **Writing Project**

Plan and Write: Blog . . . 151
Check Your Work . . . 152

Timed Reading Chart . . . 153

Decodable Stories . . . 154

Foundations of Reading

Name _____

▶ Letters and Sounds

A. Study the new letters and sounds.

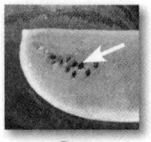

Ss

Mm

Ff

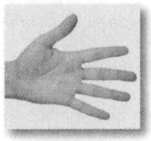

Hh

Tt

Aa

B. Say the name of each picture below. What letter spells the first sound you hear? Circle the letter.

1. 

t (h) a

2. 

a h s

3. 

h f s

4. 

f h a

5. 

a m s

6. 

t h a

7. 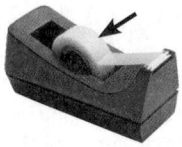

a m t

8. 

a s m

9. 

t h a

© NGSP & HB

Foundations of Reading

Name _____

▶ Letters and Sounds

Say the name of each picture below. What letter spells the first sound you hear? Write the letter.

1. 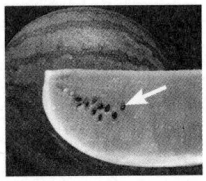

_____

2. 

_____

3. 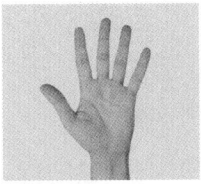

_____

4. 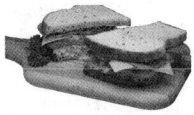

_____

5. 

_____

6. 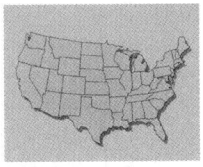

_____

7. 

_____

8. 

_____

9. 

_____

10. 

_____

11. 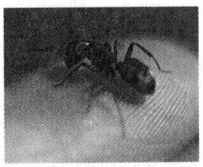

_____

12. 

_____

13. 

_____

14. 

_____

15. 

_____

© NGSP & HB

Name _____

▶ High Frequency Words

Read each word. Then write it.

1. am	_____	4. school	_____
2. I	_____	5. the	_____
3. is	_____	6. this	_____

How to Play

1. Make a spinner.
2. Write the name of each player on a blank.
3. Spin. Read the sentence.

The first player to read all six sentences wins.

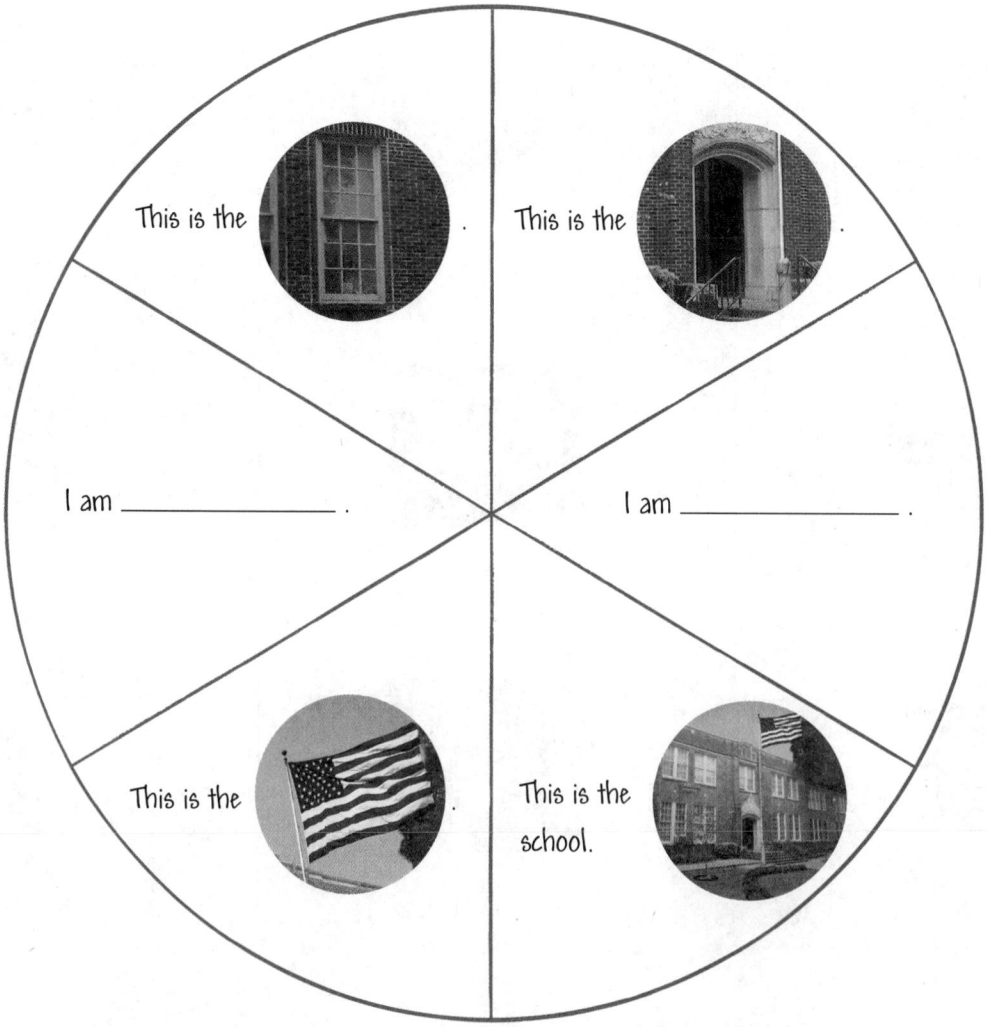

© NGSP & HB

Foundations of Reading

Name _____

▶ High Frequency Words

Read each word. Then write it.

1. a	_____	4. my	_____
2. an	_____	5. no	_____
3. here	_____	6. you	_____

1. Find the words. Circle them.
Look across. →

q	a	o	p	t	m
v	l	e	s	a	n
s	b	m	l	n	l
h	e	r	e	o	r
z	p	l	g	m	y
n	o	r	z	q	w
w	f	y	o	u	z
x	g	q	t	d	s

Write the missing words.

2. Here is my  .
(my / no)

3. Here is _____  .
(you / a)

4. _____ is a  .
(A / Here)

5. Find the words. Circle them.
Look down. ↓

a	q	h	j	z	t
n	v	e	u	n	s
k	s	r	r	o	g
l	b	e	h	o	y
r	a	i	z	e	o
x	f	s	m	r	u
w	g	o	y	e	q
p	u	z	e	l	v

Write the missing words.

6. This is an  .
(an / you)

7. _____ is a  .
(Here / My)

8. This is _____  .
(no / a)

© NGSP & HB

Foundations of Reading

Name _____

▶ High Frequency Words

A. Read each word. Then write it.

1. at	_____	4. of	_____
2. it	_____	5. on	_____
3. look	_____	6. yes	_____

B. Write the missing letters.

7. Which words have a **t**?

   a t ___ ___

8. Which words have 2 letters?

   ___ ___ ___ ___

   ___ ___ ___ ___

9. Which word has 3 letters?

   ___ ___ ___

10. Which word has 4 letters?

    ___ ___ ___ ___

11. Which words start with **o**?

    ___ ___ ___ ___

12. Which word has an **f**?

    ___ ___

C. Write the missing words.

13. Carlos, _____ at this!
    (of / look)

14. Is this the school?
    Yes, _____ is.
    (it / at)

15. I am _____ school.
    (at / of)

16. This is a 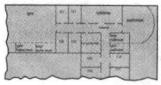 _____
    (of / look)
    the school.

17. The  is _____
    (it / on)
    the  .

© NGSP & HB

Name _____

▶ **Read on Your Own**

Read these sentences.

Sam has ham.

_____

Sam has a hat.

_____

Sam has a mat.

© NGSP & HB

Name _____

▶ Words with Short *a*

A. Read each word. Draw a line to match the word and the picture.

1.

hat

ham

2.

fat

mat

B. Write the missing words.

3.

This is a hat .
(ham / hat)

4.

Maylin is _____ school.
(at / sat)

5.

Here is the _____ .
(fat / mat)

6.

I _____ Ron.
(Sam / am)

7.

This is a _____ .
(ham / hat)

8.

You _____ at the  .
(at / sat)

© NGSP & HB

Foundations of Reading

Name _____

▶ Words with Short *a*

A. Write the missing *a*. Then read the words in each list. How are the words different?

1.

a m

S ___ m

h ___ m

2.

___ t

h ___ t

s ___ t

3.

___ t

f ___ t

m ___ t

B. What word completes each sentence and tells about the picture? Spell the word.

4.

Here is my h a t .

5.

I am ___ ___ ___ .

6.

This is a ___ ___ ___ .

7.

I am ___ ___ school.

8.

I ___ ___ Ron.

9.

I ___ ___ ___ on the  .

10.

Sam ___ ___ ___ a  .

11.

Look at the ___ ___ ___ .

12.

I ___ ___ at the  .

13.

You ___ ___ ___ at the  .

© NGSP & HB

Foundations of Reading

Name _____

▶ Letters and Sounds

A. Study the new letters and sounds.

Nn

Ll

Pp

Gg

Ii

B. Say the name of each picture below. What letter spells the first sound you hear? Circle the letter.

1. 

(n) f s

2. 

l p n

3. 

s l n

4. 

t h i

5. 

f m p

6. 

g p l

7. 

p f i

8. 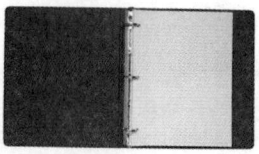

l n t

9. 

l p n

10. 

l g n

11. 

t g a

12. 

l g f

© NGSP & HB

Foundations of Reading

Name _____

▶ Letters and Sounds

Say the name of each picture below. Write the missing letters.

1.

h a m

2.

___ ___ ___

3.

___ i ___

4.

s i ___

5.

___ i ___

6.

m ___ ___

7.

___ ___ ___

8.

___ ___ m p

9.

___ ___ ___

10.

m ___ ___

11.

___ i ___

12.

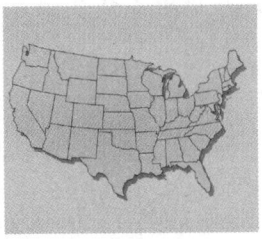

___ ___ ___

© NGSP & HB

Foundations of Reading

Name _____

▶ High Frequency Words

A. Read each word. Then write it.

1. are	_____	4. show	_____
2. good	_____	5. where	_____
3. see	_____	6. he	_____

B. Write the missing letters.

7. Which words have 4 letters?

   g o o d

   ___ ___ ___ ___

8. Which word has an **a**?

   ___ ___ ___

9. Which word has 5 letters?

   ___ ___ ___ ___ ___

10. Which words have 3 letters?

    ___ ___ ___

    ___ ___ ___

11. Which word has a **g**?

    ___ ___ ___ ___

12. Which words have a **w**?

    ___ ___ ___ ___ ___

    ___ ___ ___ ___

13. Which word has 2 letters?

    ___ ___

C. Write the missing word.

14. I _____ two pens.
    (see / are)

15. Where _____ the people?
    (are / he)

16. This is a _____ sandwich.
    (good / see)

17. _____ me the motorcycle.
    (Show / Where)

18. _____ is the boy?
    (Show / Where)

19. We do not know who _____ is.
    (see / he)

© NGSP & HB

Foundations of Reading

Name _____

▶ High Frequency Words

A. Read each word. Then write it.

1. answer	_____	4. time	_____
2. she	_____	5. who	_____
3. some	_____	6. your	_____

B. Write the missing letters.

7. Which word has 6 letters?

a ___ n ___ s ___ w ___ e ___ r ___

8. Which words have an **m**?

___ ___ ___ ___

___ ___ ___ ___

9. Which words have 3 letters?

___ ___ ___

___ ___ ___

10. Which words have 4 letters?

___ ___ ___ ___

___ ___ ___ ___

___ ___ ___ ___

11. Which words have a **w**?

___ ___ ___ ___ ___ ___

___ ___ ___

12. Which word has a **y**?

___ ___ ___ ___

C. Write the missing word.

13. I write the _____ .
(answer / some)

14. _____ is my friend.
(She / Your)

15. What _____ is class?
(time / your)

16. _____ puppy is very cute.
(Your / Who)

17. I have _____ homework.
(some / who)

18. _____ do you see?
(Who / She)

© NGSP & HB

Foundations of Reading

Name _____

▶ High Frequency Words

A. Read each word. Then write it.

1. point	_____	4. with	_____
2. read	_____	5. work	_____
3. to	_____	6. write	_____

B. Write the missing letters.

7. Which words have 4 letters?

___ ___ ___ ___

___ ___ ___ ___

___ ___ ___ ___

8. Which words have a **w**?

___ ___ ___ ___

___ ___ ___ ___

___ ___ ___ ___ ___

9. Which words have 5 letters?

___ ___ ___ ___ ___

___ ___ ___ ___ ___

10. Which word has a **k**?

___ ___ ___ ___

11. Which words have an **r**?

___ ___ ___ ___

___ ___ ___ ___

___ ___ ___ ___ ___

C. Write the missing word.

12. I _____ a book.
(read / point)

13. I _____ to the answer.
(work / point)

14. Carlos will _____ on the board.
(write / with)

15. I need _____ see you.
(point / to)

16. I will go _____ Lisa to the store.
(with / read)

17. Eli likes to _____ on computers.
(with / work)

© NGSP & HB

Name _____

▶ **Read on Your Own**

Read these sentences.

Tim has a lamp.

_____

Here is his pan.

_____

This is his pin.

_____

Here is his lid.

_____

This is Tim.

© NGSP & HB

Name _____

▶ Words with Short *a* and *i*

A. Read each word. Draw a line to match the word and the picture.

1.

pan

map

man

2.

pin

sit

pig

B. Write the missing words.

3.

She has a hat.

(hat / mat)

4.

This is a _____.

(pan / ham)

5.

This is a _____.

(fan / man)

6.

_____ it!

(Pin / Hit)

7.

This is a _____.

(pin / pig)

8.

He is a _____.

(man / mat)

9.

This is a _____.

(pan / pig)

10.

You _____

(sit / hit)

in a  .

© NGSP & HB

Foundations of Reading

Name _____

▶ Words with Short *a* and *i*

A. Write the missing letters. Then read the words in each list. How are the words different?

1.

h ___ ___

___ ___ ___

___ ___ ___

2.

p ___ ___

___ ___ ___

___ ___ ___

B. Read each question. What word goes in the answer? Spell the word.
Then circle the correct picture.

3. Where is the pig?

The p i g is here.

4. Where is the pan?

Here is the ___ ___ ___ .

5. Where is Sam?

___ ___ ___ is here.

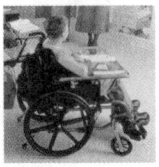

6. Who hit it?

Carlos ___ ___ ___ it.

7. Who has the hat?

She ___ ___ ___ the hat.

8. Who is the man?

He is the ___ ___ ___ .

© NGSP & HB

Foundations of Reading

Name _____

▶ Letters and Sounds

A. Study the new letters and sounds.

Rr

Dd

Cc

Vv

Oo

B. Say the name of each picture below. What letter spells the first sound you hear? Circle the letter.

1. 
m (d) o

2. 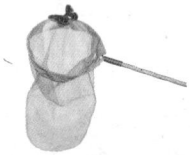
r v n

3. 
l h c

4. 
a r d

5. 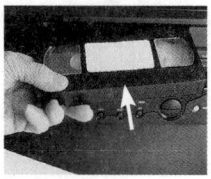
c n v

6. 
o r i

7. 
l g c

8. 
h t p

9. 
r d f

10. 
a v l

11. 
d a s

12. 
v i h

13. 
c p t

14. 
o m v

15. 
o d i

16. 
d g v

© NGSP & HB

Foundations of Reading

Name _____

▶ Letters and Sounds

Say the name of each picture below. Write the missing letters.

1. 

d o t

2. 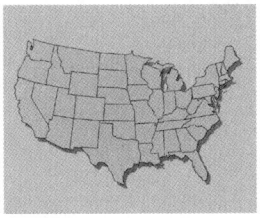

___ ___ ___

3. 

___ o ___

4. 

___ ___ ___

5. 

___ ___ ___

6. 

f l ___ ___

7. 

c l ___ s s

8. 

___ a ___

9. 

___ a ___

10. 

___ ___ m p

11. 

___ ___ ___

12. 

___ ___ ___

© NGSP & HB

Name _____

▶ High Frequency Words

Read each word. Then write it.

1. do	_____	4. help	_____
2. does	_____	5. in	_____
3. for	_____	6. like	_____

How to Play

1. Play with a partner. 

Each partner chooses a sign. X O
2. Partner 1 reads a word and marks the square with a sign. 

3. Partner 2 takes a turn. 

4. Get 3 Xs or Os in a row to win.

A.

do	help	like
in	does	for
point	read	to

B.

does	point	read
in	do	help
for	like	to

C.

help	does	do
for	like	in
with	work	write

D.

like	work	does
write	do	help
for	with	in

© NGSP & HB

Foundations of Reading

Name _____

▶ High Frequency Words

A. Read each word. Then write it.

1. around	_____	4. will	_____
2. me	_____	5. and	_____
3. picture	_____	6. don't	_____

B. Write the missing letters.

7. Which word has 3 letters?

   a n d

8. Which word is two words together?

   ___ ___ ___ ___

9. Which word has 6 letters?

   ___ ___ ___ ___ ___ ___

10. Which words have an **r**?

    ___ ___ ___ ___ ___ ___

    ___ ___ ___ ___ ___ ___ ___

11. Which word has 2 letters?

    ___ ___

12. Which words have a **d**?

    ___ ___ ___ ___ ___ ___

    ___ ___ ___

    ___ ___ ___ ___

C. Write the missing word.

13. I see your _____ in
    (picture / around)
    the yearbook.

14. Yes, I _____
    (don't / will)
    play basketball.

15. Tell _____ about
    (and / me)
    the game.

16. Can you run _____
    (around / picture)
    the track?

17. Why _____ you
    (don't / and)
    stay there?

© NGSP & HB

Foundations of Reading

Name _____

▶ High Frequency Words

A. Read each word. Then write it.

1. food	_____	4. both	_____
2. not	_____	5. get	_____
3. that	_____	6. these	_____

B. Write the missing letters.

7. Which words have 3 letters?

n o t

g e t

8. Which words have 4 letters?

___ ___ ___ ___

___ ___ ___ ___

___ ___ ___ ___

9. Which words end in **t**?

___ ___ ___

___ ___ ___

___ ___ ___ ___

10. Which words have an **e**?

___ ___ ___

___ ___ ___ ___ ___

11. Which word has 5 letters?

___ ___ ___ ___ ___

C. Write the missing word.

12. I ate the _____ .
(both / food)

13. Sam saw _____ apple.
(get / that)

14. I did _____ see the shooting star.
(get / not)

15. Did you _____ help the girl?
(both / food)

16. Did Lin _____ the ball?
(these / get)

17. We ate _____ chips.
(food / these)

© NGSP & HB

Name _____

▶ **Read on Your Own**

Read these sentences.

This dot is on a van.

_____

The dot is on a map.

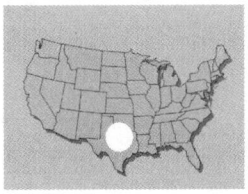

_____

The dot is on a cot.

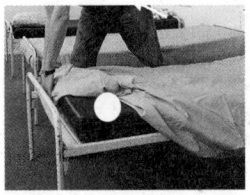

_____

The dot is on a pig.

_____

The dot is on Ron!

© NGSP & HB

Name _____

▶ Words with Short *a*, *i*, and *o*

A. Read each word. Draw a line to the correct picture.

1.

mop

map

man

2.

pan

pig

pin

3.

pot

dot

mop

B. Write the missing words.

4.

This is a

van

_____ .

(van / man)

5.

I like this

_____ .

(map / man)

6.

The _____

(pot / dot)

is hot.

7.

Here is a good

_____ .

(map / mop)

8.

This is a

_____ .

(not / dot)

9.

This lamp is

_____ .

(am / on)

© NGSP & HB

Name _____

▶ Words with Short *a*, *i*, and *o*

A. Write the missing letters. Then read the words in each list. How are the words different?

1. 
c ___ ___

___ ___ ___

___ ___ ___

2. 
p ___ ___

___ ___ ___

___ ___ ___

3. 
h ___ ___

___ ___ ___

___ ___ ___

B. Read each question and the answer. Write the missing words. Then circle the correct picture.

4. Is this pot hot?

No, the p o t is not h o t.

5. Is this your cap?

Yes, it is my ___ ___ ___.

6. Where is the mop?

The ___ ___ ___ is here.

7. Where can I sit?

You can ___ ___ ___ here.

8. Point to the dot.

The ___ ___ ___ is here!

9. Do you like the hat?

Yes, I like the ___ ___ ___.

© NGSP & HB

Name _____

▶ Letters and Sounds

Study the new letters and sounds.

Jj

Bb

Ww

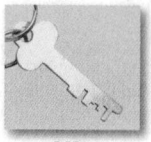
Kk

Ee

How to Play Bingo

1. Write the letters from the box. Write one letter in each square.
2. Then listen to the word your teacher reads.
3. Put a ◯ on the letter that stands for the first sound in the word.
4. The first player to cover all the letters in a row is the winner.

Letters to Write

a	i	p
b	j	r
b	j	s
c	k	t
d	k	v
e	l	w
f	m	w
g	n	
h	o	

Words to Read

am	got	lot	top
bat	hit	mat	van
big	it	not	win
can	jam	on	wig
dot	jog	pin	
egg	kid	red	
fat	kit	sit	

© NGSP & HB

Foundations of Reading

Name _____

▶ Letters and Sounds

Say the name of each picture below. Write the missing letters.

1. 

p o t

2. 

___ ___ ___

3. 

___ ___ ___

4. 

___ g g

5. 

___ e s t

6. 

___ ___ ___

7. 

___ ___ ___

8. 

___ o g

9. 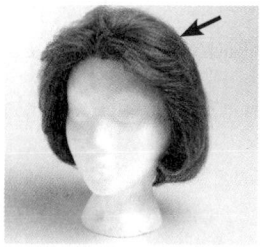

___ i g

10. 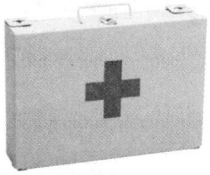

___ i t

11. 

___ e ___

12. 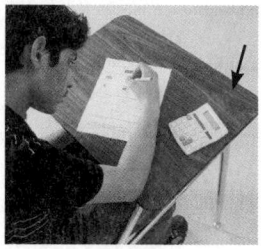

___ e ___ ___

© NGSP & HB

Name _____

▶ High Frequency Words

A. Read each word. Then write it.

1. things _____
2. little _____
3. old _____
4. them _____
5. those _____
6. very _____

B. Write the missing letters.

7. Which word has 3 letters?

   o l d

8. Which words have an **i**?

   ___ ___ ___ ___ ___ ___

   ___ ___ ___ ___ ___ ___

9. Which word has a **v**?

   ___ ___ ___ ___

10. Which words have 4 letters?

    ___ ___ ___ ___

    ___ ___ ___ ___

C. Write the missing word.

11. The food is _____ good.
    (very / little)

12. Did you see _____ bananas?
    (things / those)

13. The flea was very _____.
    (them / little)

14. I saw _____ at school.
    (them / very)

15. The _____ dog liked to sleep.
    (things / old)

16. I have many _____.
    (those / things)

© NGSP & HB

Foundations of Reading

Name _____

▶ High Frequency Words

A. Read each word. Then write it.

1. think	_____	4. which	_____
2. take	_____	5. can	_____
3. give	_____	6. play	_____

B. Write the missing letters.

7. Which words have 4 letters?

t a k e

___ ___ ___ ___

___ ___ ___ ___

___ ___ ___ ___

8. Which words have 5 letters?

___ ___ ___ ___ ___

___ ___ ___ ___ ___

9. Which word has a **g**?

___ ___ ___ ___

10. Which word has 3 letters?

___ ___ ___

11. Which words have an **a**?

___ ___ ___

___ ___ ___ ___

___ ___ ___ ___

C. Write the missing word.

12. I _____ I know the answer.
(think / play)

13. Juan _____ run very fast.
(which / can)

14. _____ your turn next.
(Take / Which)

15. Can you _____ baseball?
(can / play)

16. _____ book is yours?
(Take / Which)

17. Let's _____ food to the hamster.
(give / play)

© NGSP & HB

Foundations of Reading

Name _____

▶ High Frequency Words

A. Read each word. Then write it.

1. too	_____	4. have	_____
2. feel	_____	5. how	_____
3. has	_____	6. put	_____

B. Write the missing letters.

7. Which words have 3 letters?

t o o

___ ___ ___

___ ___ ___

___ ___ ___

___ ___ ___

8. Which words have 4 letters?

___ ___ ___ ___

___ ___ ___ ___

9. Which words have an **h**?

___ ___ ___

___ ___ ___

___ ___ ___ ___

10. Which word ends with a **t**?

___ ___ ___

11. Which word has two **e**'s?

___ ___ ___ ___

C. Write the missing word.

12. She has brown hair, _____ .
(too / how)

13. Where did you _____
(how / put)
the book?

14. Do you _____ sick today?
(have / feel)

15. She _____ a blue
(has / have)
backpack.

16. _____ are you feeling
(Have / How)
today?

17. I _____ two cookies.
(how / have)

© NGSP & HB

Name _____

▶ **Read on Your Own**

Read these sentences.

Can Ken jog?

_____

Ken can jog well.

_____

Can Ken get his bat?

_____

Ken can get his bat.

_____

Can Ken rest?

_____

No. Ken has no bed!

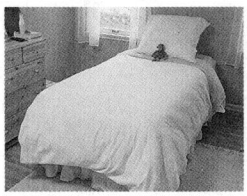

© NGSP & HB

Foundations of Reading

Name _____

▶ Words with Short *a*, *i*, *o*, and *e*

A. Read each word. Draw a line to the correct picture.

1.

jam

ham

hat

2.

pen

ten

men

3.

cat

bat

bed

B. Write the missing words.

4.

Here are two

men

(men / ten)

5.

There are

_____ dots.

(ten / pen)

6.

My pet is a

_____ .

(pig / pin)

7.

This is a good

_____ .

(pan / pen)

8.

He can _____

(hot / hit)

the ⚾.

9.

This is my

_____ .

(cap / map)

10.

Here is a

_____ .

(bed / Ed)

11.

I do _____

(dot / not)

like to play.

12.

Put it in the

_____ .

(pot / pat)

© NGSP & HB

Foundations of Reading

Name _____

▶ Words with Short *a, i, o,* and *e*

A. Write the missing letters. Then read the words in each list. How are the words different?

1.  m ___ ___

 ___ ___ ___

___ ___ ___

2.  c ___ ___

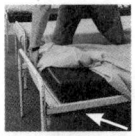 ___ ___ ___

 ___ ___ ___

3.  p ___ ___

 ___ ___ ___

 ___ ___ ___

B. Write the missing words.

4. 

This is my p e n .

5. 

Look at the

___ ___ ___ .

6. 

Here is my ___ ___ ___ .

7. 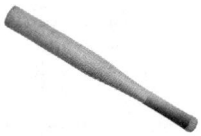

Carlos has a

___ ___ ___ .

8. 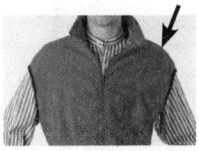

Do you like my

___ ___ s t ___ ?

9. 

This is a

f l ___ ___ .

10. 

I like to ___ ___ ___ .

11. 

I ___ ___ ___ at my desk.

12. 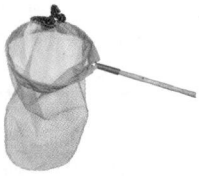

Where is my

___ ___ ___ ?

© NGSP & HB

Foundations of Reading

Name _____

▶ Letters and Sounds

Study the new letters and sounds.

Zz

Yy

Uu

Qq

Xx

How to Play Bingo

1. Write the letters from the box. Write one letter in each square.
2. Then listen to the word your teacher reads.
3. Put a ◯ on the letter that stands for the first sound in the word.
4. The first player to cover all the letters in a row is the winner.

Letters to Write

a	j	s
b	k	t
c	l	u
d	m	v
e	n	w
f	o	y
g	p	z
h	q	
i	r	

Words to Read

am	him	on	van
bat	in	pen	wig
cot	jam	quit	yes
dot	kid	red	zip
egg	lot	sat	
fan	map	ten	
got	not	up	

© NGSP & HB

Foundations of Reading

Name _____

▶ Letters and Sounds

Say the name of each picture below. Write the missing letters.

1.

l e g

2.

i l t

3.

4.

5.

6.

7.

u

8.

u

9.

10.

11.

u

12.

© NGSP & HB

Foundations of Reading

Name _____

▶ High Frequency Words

A. Read each word. Then write it.

1. they	_____	4. soon	_____
2. great	_____	5. tomorrow	_____
3. later	_____	6. call	_____

B. Write the missing letters.

7. Which words have 4 letters?

t h e y

___ ___ ___ ___

___ ___ ___ ___

8. Which words have 5 letters?

___ ___ ___ ___ ___

___ ___ ___ ___ ___

9. Which words have an **a**?

___ ___ ___ ___ ___

___ ___ ___ ___ ___

___ ___ ___ ___

10. Which word ends with a **t**?

___ ___ ___ ___ ___

11. Which word has 8 letters?

___ ___ ___ ___ ___ ___ ___ ___

C. Write the missing word.

12. I will be in class _____ .
(great / tomorrow)

13. I will see him _____,
(soon / they)
I hope!

14. Shana will be there _____ .
(later / call)

15. Did you _____ your
(call / soon)
dad yet?

16. He did _____ on the test.
(soon / great)

17. When will _____ be here?
(they / call)

© NGSP & HB

Foundations of Reading

Name _____

▶ High Frequency Words

A. Read each word. Then write it.

1. name	_____	4. we	_____
2. need	_____	5. what	_____
3. number	_____	6. book	_____

B. Write the missing letters.

7. Which word has 2 letters?

   w e

8. Which words have 4 letters?

   ___ ___ ___ ___

   ___ ___ ___ ___

   ___ ___ ___ ___

   ___ ___ ___ ___

9. Which word has 6 letters?

   ___ ___ ___ ___ ___ ___

10. Which word ends with a **t**?

    ___ ___ ___ ___

11. Which word has an **r**?

    ___ ___ ___ ___ ___ ___

C. Write the missing word.

12. What is your _____ ?
    (we / name)

13. Find the _____ ten.
    (number / book)

14. The _____ is on the shelf.
    (book / need)

15. _____ went to the library.
    (We / Number)

16. I _____ to do my homework.
    (need / what)

17. _____ did you do last week?
    (What / We)

© NGSP & HB

Name _____

▶ High Frequency Words

A. Read each word. Then write it.

1. boy _____
2. day _____
3. girl _____
4. group _____
5. letters _____
6. night _____
7. year _____

B. Write the missing letters.

8. Which word ends with a **p**?

g ___ r ___ o ___ u ___ p ___

9. Which words have 3 letters?

___ ___ ___

___ ___ ___

10. Which words have 5 letters?

___ ___ ___ ___ ___

___ ___ ___ ___ ___

11. Which word ends with **s**?

___ ___ ___ ___ ___ ___ ___

12. Which words have a **y** in them?

___ ___ ___ ___

___ ___ ___

___ ___ ___

C. Write the missing word.

13. I saw the _____ in class.
(night / boy)

14. Last _____, the sky was clear.
(group / night)

15. He has many _____ from Tom.
(letters / day)

16. During the _____ the sun is out.
(day / night)

17. The _____ plays basketball.
(year / girl)

18. There is a _____ of students.
(boy / group)

19. This _____ I am a freshman.
(night / year)

© NGSP & HB

Name _____

▶ **Read on Your Own**

Read these sentences.

My quilt is big.

My rug is not big.

This ox is big.

This pup is not big.

That bus is very big!

That ant is not very big!

© NGSP & HB

Name _____

▶ Words with Short *a, i, o, e,* and *u*

A. Read each word. Draw a line to the correct picture.

1.

cot

cat

cap

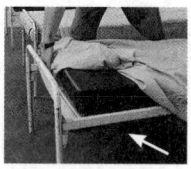

2.

up

cup

cut

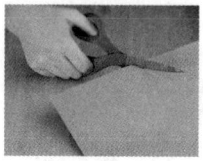

3.

ax

ox

box

B. Say the name of each picture below. Write the missing letters.

4.

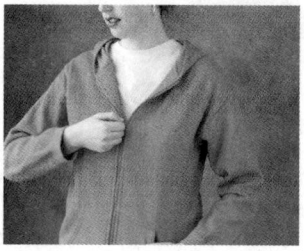

I can z i p it.

6.

I like this old

____ ____ ____ ____ ____ .

8.

I have ____ ____ ____

pins.

5.

This is my ____ ____ ____ .

7.

Do you like my little

____ ____ ____ ?

9.

Is this a pig?

____ ____ ____ !

© NGSP & HB

Foundations of Reading

Name _____

▶ Words with Short *a, i, o, e,* and *u*

A. Write the missing letters. Then read the words in each list. How are the words different?

1. u p
2. c
3. p

B. Write the missing words.

4. There is m i l k in my ___ ___ ___ .
5. Is this my ___ ___ ___ ?
6. He ___ ___ ___ it.
7. I have a ___ ___ ___ ___ ___ .
8. She can ___ ___ ___ it.
9. Here is an ___ ___ ___ .
10. There is a bug on my ___ ___ ___ .
11. He has an ___ ___ .
12. The lamp is not in the ___ ___ ___ .

© NGSP & HB

Name _____

Mind Map

Use the mind map to show what personal information is and how to share it. As you read the selections in this unit, add new ideas you learn about getting to know people.

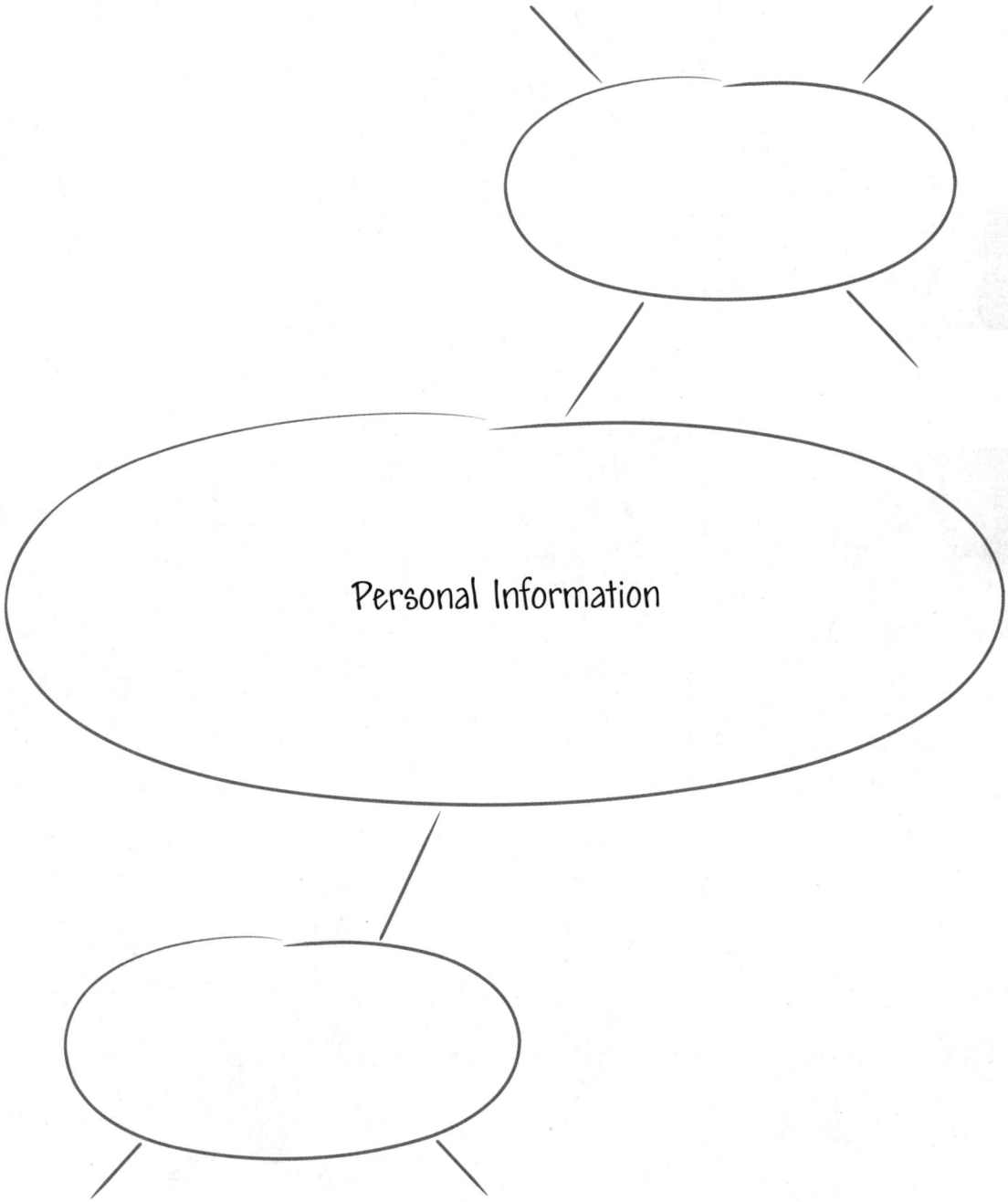

© NGSP & HB

Name _____

Use Pronouns in Greetings

▶ **Language: Exchange Greetings and Good-byes**

▶ **Grammar: Pronouns**

A. Study the chart.

Greetings and Good-byes

Greetings	Questions and Answers	Good-byes
Hi!	How are you? I am fine. We are fine, thank you.	Bye!
Hello!		Good-bye!
Good morning!		So long!
Good afternoon!	How are you today? I am okay. We are well, thanks.	Have a nice day!
Nice to meet you!		See you later!

Pronouns

Use ***I*** to talk about yourself.

I am happy.

Use ***you*** when you talk to someone else.

You are nice.

Use ***we*** to talk about yourself and someone else.

We are friends.

B. Write what the people say. Use the chart.

1.

Greetings

2.

Question and Answer

3.

Question and Answer

4.

Good-byes

© NGSP & HB

 Name _____

Who Is It?

▶ Grammar: Pronouns

When you talk about other people or things, use the correct pronoun.

For a girl or a woman, use ***she.***

She is a student.

For a thing, use ***it.***

It is a present.

For a boy or a man, use ***he.***

He is a student, too.

Use ***they*** to talk about more than one person or thing.

They are friends.

Complete each sentence. Add the correct pronoun.

1. Josef and Mikka sit together.

   They are friends.

2. Mikka is 13 years old today.

   _____ is a teenager now.

3. Josef has a present for Mikka.

   _____ is a good friend.

4. Mikka likes surprises.

   _____ takes the present.

5. The present makes Mikka smile.

   _____ is a CD by her favorite band.

6. The friends laugh.

   _____ are happy.

© NGSP & HB

Language Development

Name _____

They Are in a Race

▶ Grammar: Present Tense Verbs: *Am, Is,* and *Are*

Use the verbs *am*, *is*, and *are* correctly.

Pronoun	Verb	Example
I	am	I **am** in P.E. class.
he she it	is	He **is** slow. She **is** in front of me. It **is** a nice day.
we you they	are	We **are** happy. You **are** fast! They **are** outside.

Complete each sentence. Add the correct verb.

1. 

I ___am___ Lisa.

2. 

She _____ in this race, too.

3. 

He _____ behind us.

4. 

I _____ not as fast as Jan.

5. 

We say, "You _____ the winner, Jan!"

6. 

Now we _____ ready to rest.

© NGSP & HB

Name _____

How Can You Communicate?

▶ **Vocabulary: Communication**

▶ **Language: Use the Telephone**

A. Name each picture. Use words from the box.

letter	fax	phone	e-mail

1. 

e-mail

2. 

_____

3. 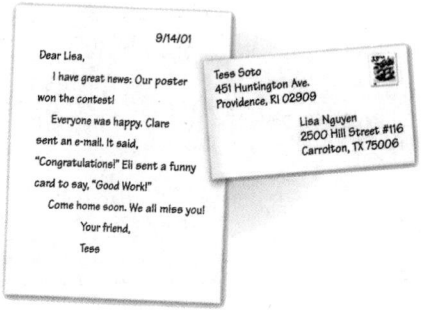

_____

4. 

_____

B. You call Sam on the phone. Write what you say.

5. **You:** Hi, Sam. This is _____ .

   Sam: Hello. How are you?

6. **You:** I am fine, thanks. How can I order a school _____ ?

   Sam: Send me an e-mail.

7. **You:** I do not have e-mail. Can I send you a _____ ?

   Sam: Sure. Tell the size and color you need.

8. **You:** Okay. Thanks for your help. _____ !

   Sam: You are welcome. See you tomorrow!

© NGSP & HB

 Name _____

Identify Sequence

▶ Sum It Up

A. Read about good news. Then make a sequence chain. Tell who gets the good news and how they get it. Tell about events in order.

Good News from Manuel

Marta gets a letter from Cousin Manuel. It is good news! Cousin Manuel is coming to visit!

Marta sends an e-mail to her brother Rico to tell him the good news. Rico sends a fax to Grandfather to tell him the good news. Grandfather calls Uncle Ciro on the phone to tell him the good news. The good news travels fast!

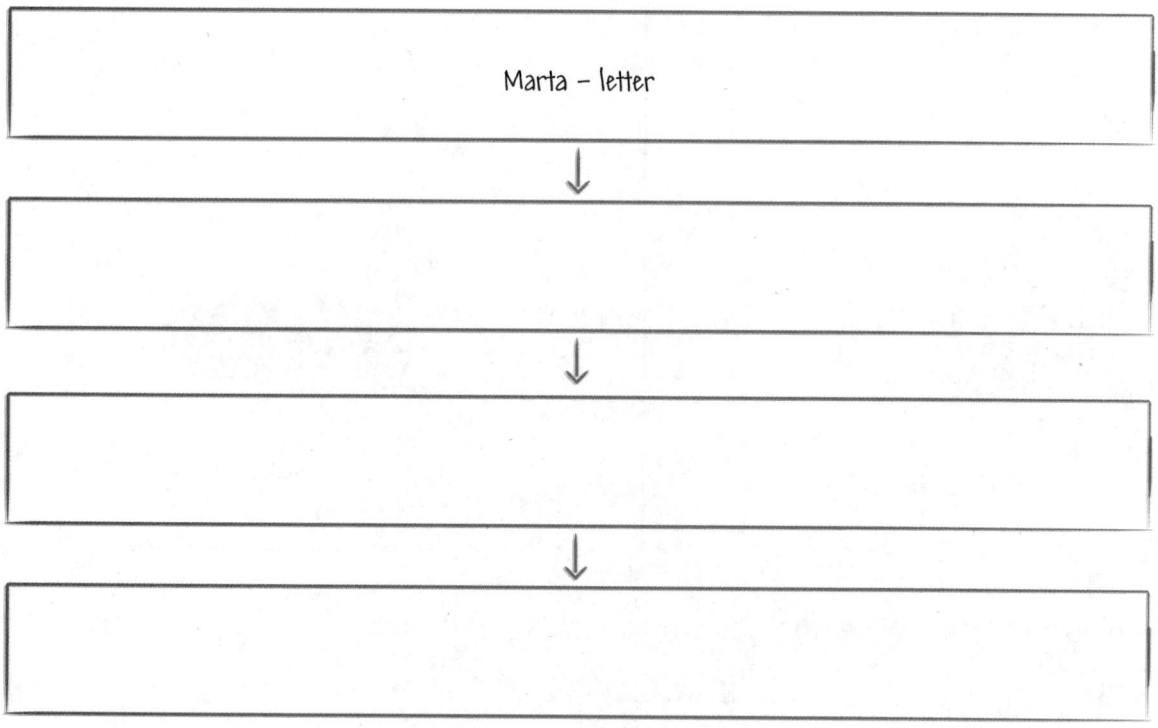

B. Read each question. Write the answers.

1. What is the good news? _____
2. Who gets the news first? _____
3. Does Grandfather or Uncle Ciro get the news from Rico? _____
4. Who gets the news last? _____

© NGSP & HB

Name _____

High Frequency Words, Part 1

A. Read each word. Then write it.

1. from _____
2. home _____
3. new _____
4. go _____
5. there _____

B. Read each sentence. Find the new words in the box. Write the words on the lines.

6. These two words have an **m**.

   from _____ _____

7. This word has 3 letters.

   _____

8. This word is the opposite of **stop**.

   _____

9. This word rhymes with **where**.

   _____

10. This word starts with **fr**.

    _____

© NGSP & HB

Name _____

High Frequency Words, Part 2

A. Read each word. Then write it.

1. many _____
2. first _____
3. next _____
4. then _____
5. one _____

B. Read each sentence. Find the new words in the box. Write the words on the lines.

6. This word has an **m**.

   many

7. These 3 words tell "when."

   _____ _____ _____

8. This word has 3 letters.

   _____

9. These 3 words have 4 letters each.

   _____ _____ _____

10. This word has an **o**.

    _____

© NGSP & HB

Name _____

Words with Short *a* and Short *o*

A. Name each picture. Write the name.

1. 

clock

2. 

_____

3. 

_____

4. 

_____

5. 

_____

6. 

_____

7. 

_____

8. 

_____

B. Now read the story. Circle the words with short *a* or short *o*. Write them in the chart. Write each word one time.

Cat Fun

Sam has a cat.

The cat has lots of fun.

It hops on the hat.

It naps in a pot.

It got into a pan.

It sleeps on the van.

When the cat is hot,

It jumps on the cot.

The cat can be bad.

But Sam likes his cat!

9. cat	18. _____
10. _____	19. _____
11. _____	20. _____
12. _____	21. _____
13. _____	22. _____
14. _____	23. _____
15. _____	24. _____
16. _____	
17. _____	

© NGSP & HB

Name _____

Words with Short *a* and Short *o*

A. Name each picture. Write the name.

1. 

hat

2. 

_____

3. 

_____

4. 

_____

5. 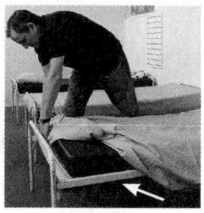

_____

6. 

_____

7. 

_____

8. 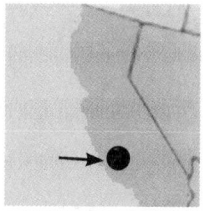

_____

B. Now read the story. Circle the words with short *a* or short *o*. Write them in the chart. Write each word one time.

I See a Van

I see a van.

It has a lot of things in it!

I see a map and a box in the van.

I see a mop and a fan in the van.

I see some pots and pans, too.

Is Tom in the van?

Tom is not in the van. There is no room!

	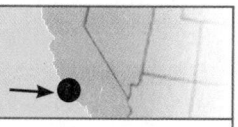
9. van	15. _____
10. _____	16. _____
11. _____	17. _____
12. _____	18. _____
13. _____	19. _____
14. _____	20. _____

© NGSP & HB

Name _____

Build Reading Fluency

▶ Expression

A. Some sentences tell something. Other sentences show strong feeling.

This sentence tells something.
It ends with a period.

Lupe is new at Lakeside School .

This sentence shows a strong feeling.
It ends with an exclamation mark.

Lupe is glad to have 2 new friends !

B. Listen to the different kinds of sentences.

New at School

Lupe is new at Lakeside School.
First she has science lab with Pat and Ron.
Pat helps Lupe.
They have many things to do.
Next they have P.E. class.
They go from one class to the next.
Pat and Lupe go fast. Ron does not go fast.
He has a cold and has to stop!
Then Pat, Lupe, and Ron go to lunch.
They have a lot of hot soup there.
At last it is time to go home.
Lupe is glad to have 2 new friends!

C. Now read the sentences above. Work with a partner. Say each kind of sentence with the right expression. See how your reading improves!

© NGSP & HB

Name _____

Everything Is New!

▶ Statements and Exclamations

A. Some sentences tell something. Other sentences show a strong feeling.

This sentence tells something. It ends with a period.

Vu has a new jacket .

All sentences start with a capital letter.

She goes to a new school today.

This sentence shows a strong feeling. It ends with an exclamation mark.

She loves it !

B. Complete each sentence. Start each sentence with a capital letter. Add a period or an exclamation mark at the end.

1. Vu opens her new locker.
   (Vu)
2. It is very small _____
3. She puts her jacket in it _____

4. Vu meets her new teacher _____
5. _____ teaches English.
   (he)
6. He is very tall _____

7. Vu walks home _____
8. _____ sees snow for the first time.
   (she)
9. She loves the snow _____
10. This is a great day _____

© NGSP & HB

Learn Key Vocabulary

Name _____

Many People to Meet: Key Vocabulary

A. Study each word. Circle a number to rate how well you know it. Then complete the chart.

Rating Scale	1	2	3
	I have never seen this word before.	I am not sure of the word's meaning.	I know this word and can teach the word's meaning to someone else.

▲ There are many **people** to **meet** in your neighborhood.

Key Words	Check Understanding	Deepen Understanding
1 first (furst) *adverb* **Rating:** 1 2 3	If you are **first**, you are at the end of the line. **Yes** **No**	What is the first thing you say when you see a friend? _____ _____ _____ _____
2 home (hōm) *noun* **Rating:** 1 2 3	A **home** can be a house or apartment. **Yes** **No**	Describe your home. _____ _____ _____ _____
3 meet (mēt) *verb* **Rating:** 1 2 3	When you **meet** a friend for lunch, you sit together and talk while you eat. **Yes** **No**	Where do you meet friends? _____ _____ _____ _____

© NGSP & HB

Name _____

You **meet people** at school every day! ▶

Key Words	Check Understanding	Deepen Understanding
❹ **next** (nekst) *adverb* **Rating:** 1 2 3	I mail a letter. I put a stamp on it **next**. **Yes** **No**	Suppose you are next. How many people are in front of you? _____ _____ _____ _____
❺ **people** (pē-pul) *noun* **Rating:** 1 2 3	Boys and girls are **people**. **Yes** **No**	Name three people in your class. _____ _____ _____ _____

B. Use at least two of the Key Vocabulary words. Tell about a day when you met someone for the first time.

_____

_____

_____

© NGSP & HB

Writing Project

Name _____

Plan and Write

1. Who will you write to? What do you want to say? Make a list of names and possible topics.

Names	Topics
_____	_____
_____	_____
_____	_____

2. Choose a focus. Circle one name and topic.

Turn your ideas into sentences. Write your e-mail.

3. Fill in your friend's name after To:
4. Fill in your name after From:
5. Fill in the date after Sent:
6. Fill in the topic after Subject:
7. Write a greeting.
8. Write your message. Share your news.
9. Write a closing like *Love*, *See you soon*, or *Your friend*. Use a comma after the closing.
10. Write your name.

To: _____

From: _____

Sent: _____

Subject: _____

Hi _____,

How are you? I am _____. I have news for you.

I _____

_____

_____

_____

_____

© NGSP & HB

Name _____

Check Your Work

Mark Your Changes

∧ **Add.**

≡ **Capitalize.**

▶ Capitalization and End Marks

Read the e-mail. Fix capital letters and end punctuation as needed. Mark your changes. Then write the sentences correctly.

To: robert@teenschool.com
From: Luis
Sent: October 5, 2008
Subject: My soccer team

Hi Robert,

How are you? I am great I joined a soccer team at school. We are called the Wildcats. We practice three times a week We had our first game last Wednesday. our team won 2 to 1. I scored one point! I wish you were on my team write back soon.

Your friend,

Luis

_____

_____

_____

_____

_____

_____

_____

_____

_____

_____

_____

© NGSP & HB

Name _____

Mind Map

Use the mind map to show what you know about food. As you read the selections in this unit, add new ideas you learn about different types of food.

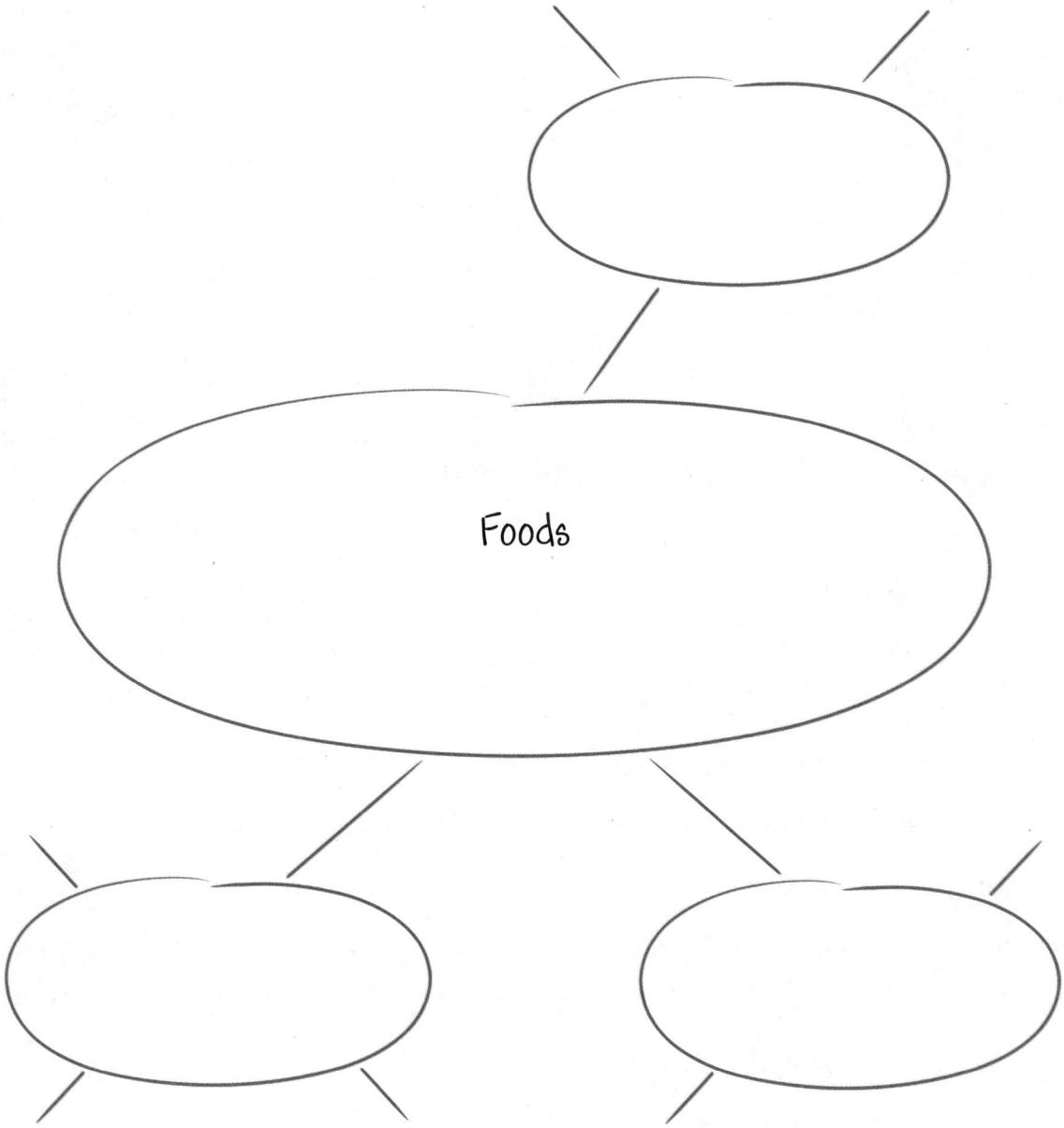

© NGSP & HB

Language Development

Name _____

Lunch Looks Good!

▶ **Vocabulary: Colors, Shapes, and Sizes**

▶ **Language: Describe**

A. Look at each picture. Tell the size or shape. Use a word from the box.

small	round	square	long	triangular	rectangular

1. 

round

2. 

_____

3. 

_____

4. 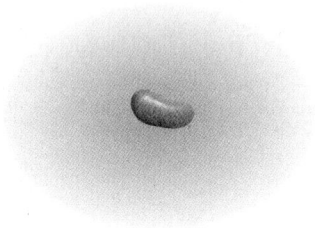

_____

5. 

_____

6. 

_____

B. Complete the sentences. Add words to tell the color, size, or shape.

7. I eat pizza with my friends. We sit at a rectangular table.
8. The pizza box has four equal sides. The box is _____ .
9. We do not eat a small pizza. We eat a _____ pizza.
10. The pizza is like a circle. It is _____ .
11. There is cheese on our pizza. The color is _____ , like a banana.
12. My slice of pizza is like a triangle. It is _____ .

© NGSP & HB

Name _____

What's for Lunch?

- **Vocabulary: Foods**
- **Language: Describe**

A. Name each food. Use words from the box.

butter	chicken	milk	plum	pear	peas	roll	water

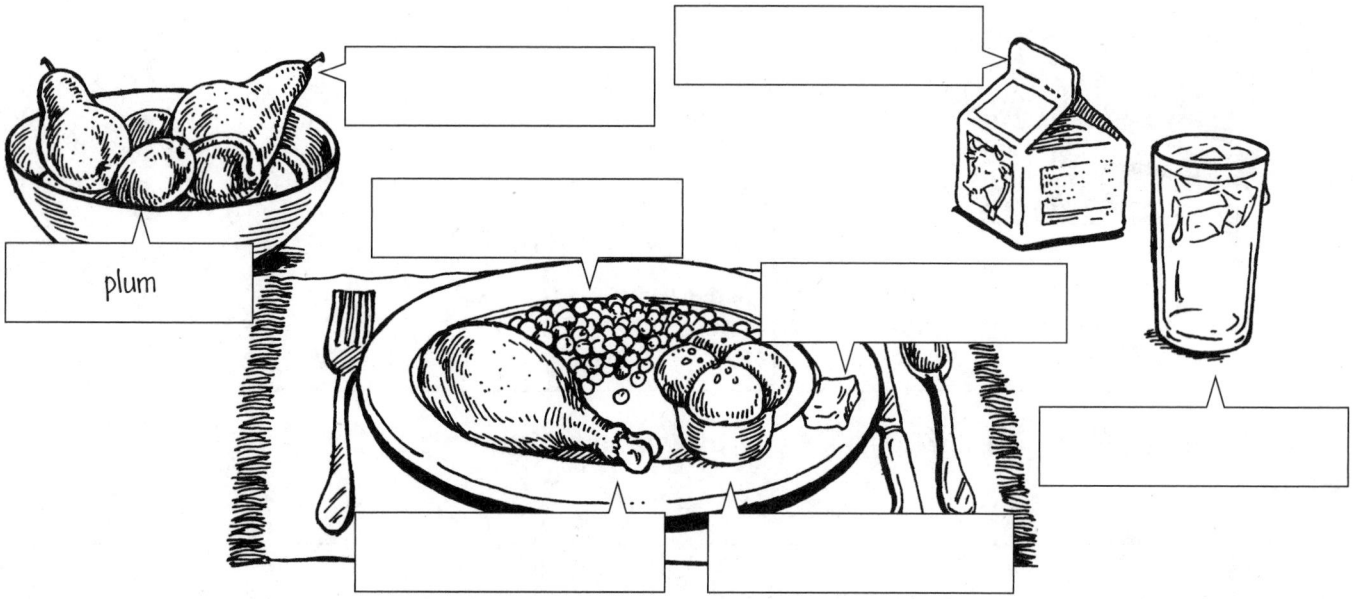

B. Complete each sentence. Tell about the food. Then name it.

1. 

This is a kind of bread. You can put butter on it. It is a roll.

2. 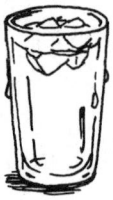

This is a cold drink. It is in a tall _____ . It is _____ .

3. 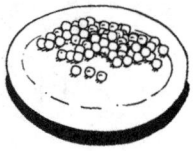

These are green. They are _____ in size. They are _____ .

4. 

This is a fruit. It has a _____ shape. It is a _____ .

© NGSP & HB

 Name _____

Let's Eat Salad

▶ Grammar: Action Verbs

An action verb tells what someone does.

I **make** tasty salads.

I **find** fresh lettuce.

I **take** a red tomato.

I **get** some carrots, too.

Action Verbs

wash	cut	eat	add	put	get

Complete each sentence. Tell how to make a salad. Use verbs from the box.

1. 

I ___wash___ the lettuce.

2. 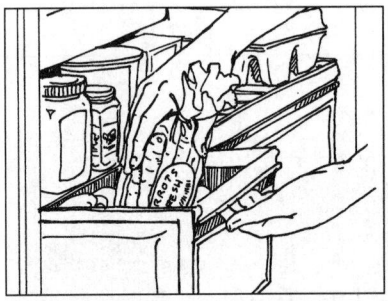

I _____ some carrots.

3. 

I _____ the tomato.

4. 

I _____ the salad in a bowl.

5. 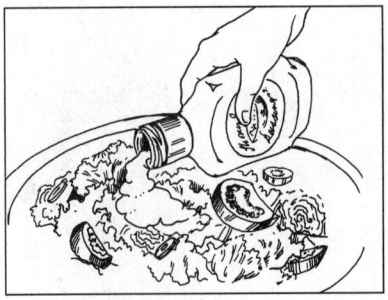

I _____ the dressing.

6. 

I _____ the salad!

© NGSP & HB

Name _____

Identify Steps in a Process

▶ Sum It Up

A. Think about how to make a hamburger. Put the steps in order.

_____ Put the burger on a bun.

_____ Shape the meat into a round burger.

_____ Cook the burger.

_1_ Put meat, onions, egg, salt, and pepper in a bowl.

_____ Mix the ingredients together.

B. Use the steps to make a sequence chain. Tell about how to make a hamburger.

Put meat, onions, egg, salt, and pepper in a bowl.

↓

↓

↓

↓

© NGSP & HB

Name _____

High Frequency Words, Part 1

A. Read each word. Then write it.

1. something _____
2. make _____
3. long _____
4. large _____
5. move _____

B. Read the clue. Write the word in the chart. Then write the word again in the sentence.

What to Look For	Word	Sentence
6. has the word **some** in it	s o m e t h i n g	I want something hot.
7. rhymes with **take**	___ ___ ___ ___	You _____ great food.
8. rhymes with **song**	___ ___ ___ ___	I like _____ noodles.
9. means "big"	___ ___ ___ ___ ___	You have a _____ bag.
10. ends with **ve**	___ ___ ___ ___	Please _____ over.

© NGSP & HB

Name _____

High Frequency Words, Part 2

A. Read each word. Then write it.

1. different _____
2. small _____
3. open _____
4. same _____
5. eat _____

B. Read the clue. Write the word in the chart. Then write the word again in the sentence.

What to Look For	Word	Sentence
6. has **ff**	d i f f e r e n t	Your bag is different.
7. starts with **sm**	___ ___ ___ ___ ___	My lunch is in a _____ bag.
8. starts with **o**	___ ___ ___ ___	I _____ my lunch bag.
9. ends with **me**	___ ___ ___ ___	Our food is not the _____.
10. has three letters	___ ___ ___	It is time to _____.

© NGSP & HB

Name _____

Words with Short *i* and Short *u*

A. Name each picture. Write the name.

1. 

pig

2. 

_____

3. 

_____

4. 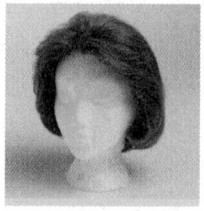

_____

5. 

_____

6. 

_____

7. 

_____

8. 

_____

B. Now read the story. Circle the words with short *i* or short *u*. Write them in the chart. Write each word one time.

My New Pup

Yesterday I got a new pup.
She sips milk from a little cup.
We sit in the sun.
Then we go for a run.
I know one day my pup will get big.
I hope she never looks like a pig!
For now I just love my silly mutt.

9. _____	15. pup
10. _____	16. _____
11. _____	17. _____
12. _____	18. _____
13. _____	19. _____
14. _____	20. _____
	21. _____
	22. _____
	23. _____

© NGSP & HB

Name _____

Words with Short *i* and Short *u*

A. Name each picture. Write the name.

1. 

pin

2. 

_____

3. 

_____

4. 

_____

5. 

_____

6. 

_____

7. 

_____

8. 

_____

B. Now read the story. Circle the words with short *i* or short *u*. Write them in the chart. Write each word one time.

Just Great!

Sam needs something to eat.
He rips open a bag of chips.
The chips are good, but not great.
Sam cuts a bit of ham and
slaps it on a bun.
The ham is good, but not great.
Mom comes in.
She gets a cup of ice cream.
She adds lots of nuts.
Sam grins. Yes! That is great!

	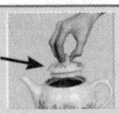
9. Just	15. _____
10. _____	16. _____
11. _____	17. _____
12. _____	18. _____
13. _____	19. _____
14. _____	20. _____
	21. _____

© NGSP & HB

Name _____

Words with Short *i* and Short *u*

A. Read each word. Which picture goes with the word? Write its letter.

1. cup G
2. fin ___
3. pump ___
4. hit ___
5. sit ___
6. rug ___
7. disk ___
8. nut ___
9. pig ___
10. dig ___
11. sun ___
12. pin ___
13. cut ___
14. lid ___
15. bun ___

A. 

B. 

C. 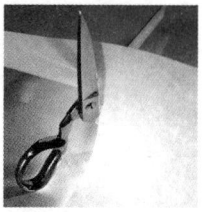

D. 

E. 

F. 

G. 

H. 

I. 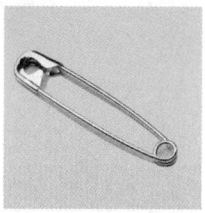

J. 

K. 

L. 

M. 

N. 

O. 

B. Name each picture below. Which word or words above rhyme with the picture name? Write the words on the lines.

16.  bun _____

17.  _____ _____

18.  _____ _____

19.  _____

20.  _____

21.  _____ _____

22. 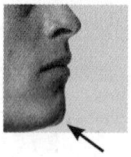 _____ _____

© NGSP & HB

Name _____

Words with Short *i* and Short *u*

A. Write the missing letters. Then read the words in each list. How are the words different?

1.

p _____ _____

_____ _____ _____

_____ _____ _____

2.

_____ _____ _____

_____ _____

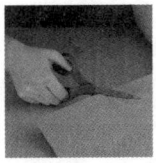

_____ _____ _____

B. Read each question. What word goes in the answer? Spell the word. Then circle the correct picture.

3. Where is the cup? The c _____ _____ is here.

4. Who made a hit? John made a _____ _____ _____.

5. Where is the first-aid kit? The first-aid _____ _____ _____ is here.

6. Where is the pup? The _____ _____ _____ is here.

7. Who can zip it? The girl can _____ _____ _____ it.

8. Where is the fish? Here is the _____ _____ _____ _____.

© NGSP & HB

Name _____

Build Reading Fluency

▶ Phrasing

A. When you read, pause between groups of words that go together.

Kim likes hot dogs / for lunch.
She cooks / a batch of hot dogs / in a big pot.

B. Listen to the story. Which groups of words does the reader say together? Where does he pause? When you hear a pause, write a /.

Example: Kim likes hot dogs / for lunch.

Something Good for Lunch

Kim likes hot dogs for lunch.
She cooks a batch of hot dogs in a big pot.
Next Kim chops some small onions.
She opens a large bag of buns.
She fills the buns with hot dogs, mustard, and onions.
She opens a bag of chips, too.
She pours a cup of punch.
This is too much food to eat!
Kim calls Mitch.
Then they sit and eat a great lunch!

B. Now read the story to a partner. Read groups of words together. Pause when you see a /.

© NGSP & HB

Name _____

I Am Not a Cook!

▶ Negative Sentences

A. A negative sentence has a negative word, like *not*.

The fish is **not** big.
The carrots are **not** long.
Meg is **not** happy.

B. Look at each picture. Complete the sentence.
Add a verb and the word *not*.

1. 

I ___am___ ___not___ a good cook.

2. 

The forks _____ _____ clean.

3. 

The plates _____ _____ on the table.

4. 

The pasta _____ _____ in the water.

5. 

The rolls _____ _____ hot.

6. 

Dinner _____ _____ ready!

© NGSP & HB

Learn Key Vocabulary

Name _____

U.S. Tour of Food: Key Vocabulary

A. Study each word. Circle a number to rate how well you know it. Then complete the chart.

Rating Scale	1	2	3
	I have never seen this word before.	I am not sure of the word's meaning.	I know this word and can teach the word's meaning to someone else.

▲ Fruit comes in different **colors, shapes,** and **sizes.**

Key Words	Check Understanding	Deepen Understanding
1 color (**kuh**-ler) *noun* **Rating:** 1 2 3	Purple is a dark **color**. **Yes** **No**	What color do you like best? _____ _____ _____ _____
2 foods (**fūdz**) *noun* **Rating:** 1 2 3	Paper and pens are **foods**. **Yes** **No**	Name two foods that you like a lot. _____ _____ _____ _____
3 shapes (**shāps**) *noun* **Rating:** 1 2 3	Apples and oranges have round **shapes**. **Yes** **No**	Name some shapes. _____ _____ _____ _____

© NGSP & HB

Name _____

There are many kinds of **foods** at a farmers' market. ▶

Key Words	Check Understanding	Deepen Understanding
4 sizes (sīzez) *noun* **Rating:** 1 2 3	Grapes and shrimp have small **sizes**. **Yes** **No**	What are some sizes of nuts? _____ _____ _____ _____
5 visit (vi-zit) *verb* **Rating:** 1 2 3	Friends may **visit** each other. **Yes** **No**	What people do you visit? _____ _____ _____ _____

B. Use at least two of the Key Vocabulary words. Describe foods you ate at your last meal.

_____

_____

_____

© NGSP & HB

Writing Project

Name _____

Plan and Write

1. What art can you make with food? Make a list. Draw pictures of what the food will look like.

Food: _____	Food: _____	Food: _____

2. Choose one idea for your How-To Card. Put a check mark next to the one you choose.
3. Think about the food you need. Plan each step. Write each step.

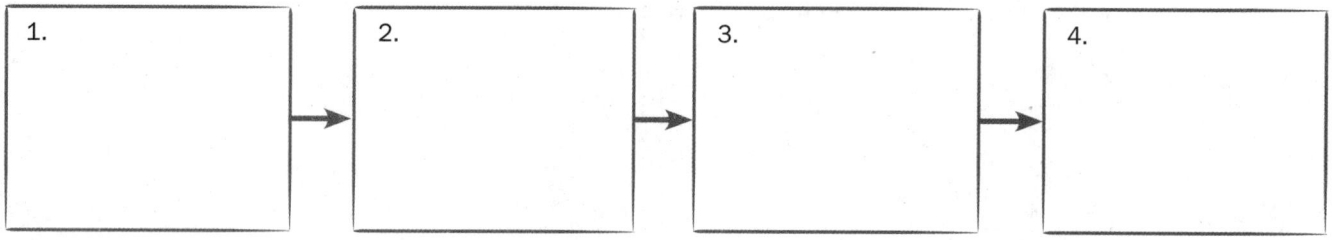

4. Fill in the title.
5. Write the steps. Use adjectives and action verbs.

How to Make _____

1. I get _____
2. I _____
3. I _____
4. I _____
5. I _____

© NGSP & HB

Name _____

Check Your Work

Mark Your Changes

∧ **Add.**

≡ **Capitalize.**

▶ Capitalization and Adding Words

Read the How-To Card. Fix capital letters. Add an action verb if one is missing from a step. Add adjectives to tell color, shape, or how many. Mark your changes.

How to Make a Rabbit Face

1. i put a pear half on a plate.
2. then I add peach slices for ears.
3. I coconut for the rabbit's fur.
4. I put raisins for eyes.
5. last, I add a cherry for the nose.

Draw a picture of what the finished rabbit face might look like.

© NGSP & HB

Name _____

Mind Map

Use the mind map to show workers at school, their jobs, and the tools they use to do their jobs. As you read the selections in this unit, add new ideas you learn about the work that people do.

Worker	Job	Tools

© NGSP & HB

Language Development

Name _____

Tell About the Jobs They Do

▶ **Language: Give Information**

▶ **Vocabulary: Actions and Careers**

A. Study the charts.

Careers	Actions
artist	draw
cab driver	drive
carpenter	build

Careers	Actions
gardener	plant
police officer	protect
teacher	teach

B. Complete each sentence. Use the chart.

1. 

He is an artist.

He can draw and paint.

2. 

She is a _____.

She can _____ things.

3. 

Here is a _____.

She can _____ flowers.

4. 

She can _____ us.

She is a _____.

5. 

He is a _____.

He can _____ us how to write.

6. 

This is a _____.

He can _____ people places.

© NGSP & HB

Name _____

Everyone Helps

▶ Grammar: Present Tense Verbs

To tell what another person or thing does, use a verb that ends in **-s**.

The Ali family **owns** a store.

It **keeps** them busy.

Mr. Ali **works** hard.

Mrs. Ali **helps**.

Read each sentence. Add the correct form of the action verb.

1.

Mr. Ali cleans .
(clean)

He _____ the sidewalk.
(sweep)

2.

He _____ a box for Mr. Ali.
(move)

It _____ fresh apples.
(hold)

3.

Mrs. Ali _____ the money.
(take)

She _____ the man.
(thank)

4.

Kira _____ a flower.
(cut)

She _____ it in water.
(put)

© NGSP & HB

Name _____

What Tools Do They Use?

▶ **Vocabulary: Tools and Careers**

▶ **Language: Ask and Answer Questions**

A. Name the tool each worker has. Use words from the box.

brush	pencil	notebook	wrench	paper	computer	scissors

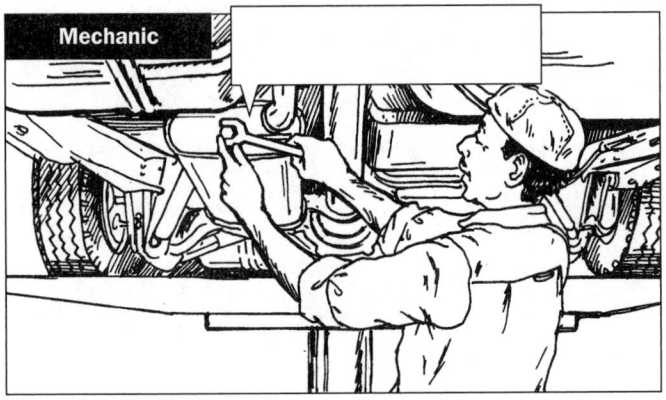

B. Look at the pictures above. Read each question. Write the answer.

1. Can the artist draw?

   Yes, she can.

2. Is the writer in an office?

   _____

3. Are the stylist and the boy in a garage?

   _____

4. Is the notebook open?

   _____

5. Can the mechanic use a wrench?

   _____

6. Is the wrench on the floor?

   _____

© NGSP & HB

 Name _____

Identify Details

▶ Sum It Up

A. Read about Hana's morning. Then make a concept web to show the people who help her.

Hana's Helpers

Hana is in a hurry to get to class. She leaves her library book on the bus. The bus driver finds the book. He gives it to the custodian. The custodian takes the book to the school office. An office worker takes the book to Hana's teacher.

Hana's teacher gives the book back to Hana. Hana is happy to get the book! That afternoon, Hana takes the book to the library. The librarian helps Hana renew the book so she can finish reading it.

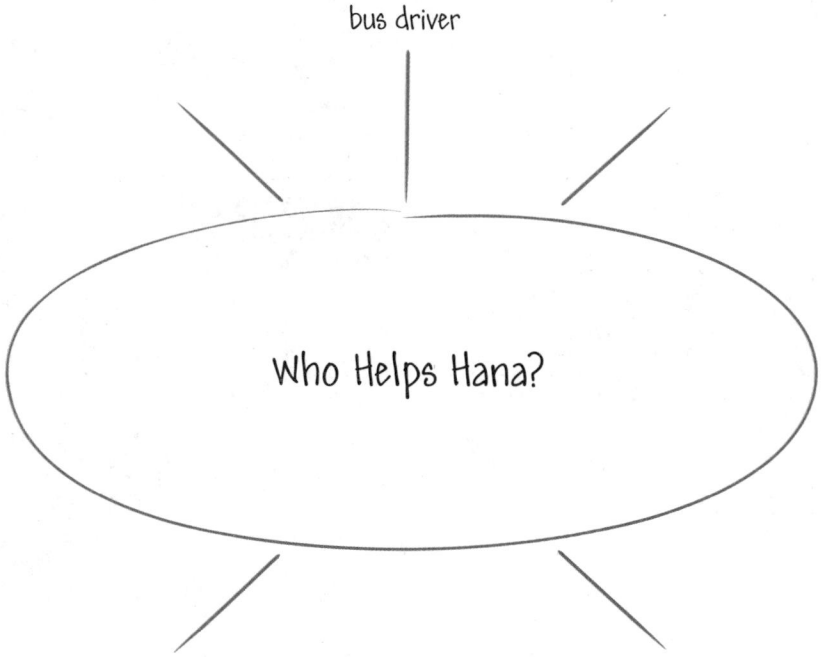

B. Finish the paragraph. Use details from your concept web.

Hana wants to thank everyone who helped her. She starts by thanking the librarian who helps her renew the book. Then Hana goes to the classroom and thanks her _____. As Hana gets on the bus to go home, she thanks the _____. The next morning, Hana thanks the _____ and the _____ at school.

© NGSP & HB

Name _____

High Frequency Words, Part 1

A. Read each word. Then write it.

1. study _____
2. learn _____
3. carry _____
4. find _____
5. use _____

B. Read each sentence. Find the new words in the box. Write the words on the lines.

6. This word starts with **st**.

   study

7. This word starts with **l**.

   _____

8. These 3 words have 5 letters each.

   _____ _____ _____

9. This word has an **i**.

   _____

10. This word ends with **e**.

    _____

© NGSP & HB

Name _____

High Frequency Words, Part 2

A. Read each word. Then write it.

1. love _____
2. face _____
3. when _____
4. want _____
5. say _____

B. Read each sentence. Find the new words in the box. Write the words on the lines.

6. This word starts with **l**.

   love

7. These 2 words end with **e**.

   _____ _____

8. This word rhymes with **then**.

   _____

9. This word ends with **nt**.

   _____

10. This word rhymes with **day**.

    _____

© NGSP & HB

Name _____

Words with Short e

A. Read each word. Which picture goes with the word? Write its letter.

1. web G
2. fence ___
3. bell ___
4. desk ___
5. ten ___
6. hen ___
7. egg ___
8. vest ___
9. leg ___

A. 

B. 

C. 

D. 

E. 

F. 

G. 

H. 

I. 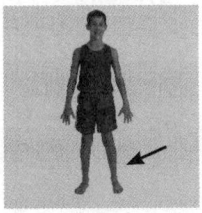

B. Read each sentence. Write the correct word on the line.

10. This word rhymes with **best**.

_____

11. This word rhymes with **tell**.

_____

© NGSP & HB

Name _____

Words with Short e

A. Read each word. Which picture goes with the word? Write its letter.

1. hen F
2. check ___
3. net ___
4. pet ___
5. bed ___
6. chest ___
7. pen ___
8. vet ___
9. egg ___
10. bench ___
11. stretch ___
12. send ___

A. 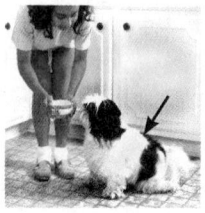

B. 

C. 

D. 

E. 

F. 

G. 

H. 

I. 

J. 

K. 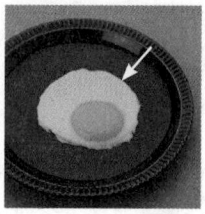

L. 

B. Name each picture below. Which words above rhyme with the picture name? Write the words on the lines.

13. 

pet _____

_____

_____

14. 

_____

_____

© NGSP & HB

Name _____

Final *ll, ss, zz, ck*

A. Read each word. Which picture goes with the word? Write its letter.

1. chick A
2. pill ___
3. bell ___
4. fizz ___
5. check ___
6. jazz ___
7. kiss ___
8. spill ___
9. rock ___
10. sick ___
11. dress ___
12. hill ___

A.

B.
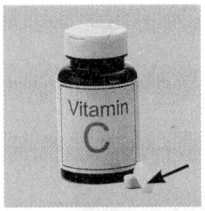

C.

D.

E.

F.

G.
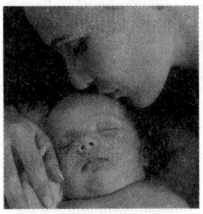

H.

I.

J.

K.

L.

B. Name each picture below. What is the last sound? Find the words above that have the same sound at the end. Write the words on the lines.

13.

pill
_____
_____
_____

14.

_____
_____
_____
_____

© NGSP & HB

Name _____

Words with *sh*

A. Read each word. Which picture goes with the word? Write its letter.

1. shirt B
2. fish ___
3. trash ___
4. ship ___
5. shell ___
6. shoulder ___

A. 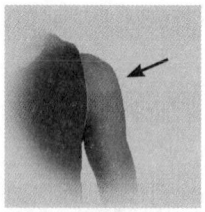

B. 

C. 

D. 

E. 

F. 

B. Now read the story. Circle the words with the *sh* sound. Write the words in the chart. Write each word one time.

Shiny New Shoes

I have a pair of shiny new shoes. They are a pale shade of blue. I think the shoelaces are too short. After school, I will take them back to the shop. I will show the laces to the salesman. I will not be shy. Tonight I will put my new shoes on a shelf. I will shut the door and go to sleep.

7. shiny	12. _____
8. _____	13. _____
9. _____	14. _____
10. _____	15. _____
11. _____	16. _____

© NGSP & HB

Name _____

Build Reading Fluency

▶ Intonation

A. Some sentences ask something. Other sentences show strong feeling.

This sentence asks a question.
It ends with a question mark.

Do you want to send something ?

This sentence shows a strong feeling.
It ends with an exclamation mark.

Then he hops on his bike and … zip !

B. Listen to the reader's voice. Listen for sentences that ask a question or show a strong feeling.

Let Ben Take It

Ben is a bike messenger.
Do you want to send something?
Ben can get it there fast.
Just say where it must go.
He gets his map.
He can study it to learn the best route.
He uses it to find a shop.
Then he hops on his bike and … zip!
He is off like a jet.
Ben can carry a lot of different things:
food, pictures, letters, flowers.
They fit in the big bag on his back.
Ben loves his job.
He has a smile on his face.
When you want to send something,
let Ben take it!

C. Now read the sentences to a partner. See how your reading improves!

© NGSP & HB

Name _____

Who? What? Where? When?

▶ Questions with *Who, What, Where,* and *When*

A. You can use the words *Who, What, Where,* or *When* to start a question.

Use *Who* to ask about a person.

Who is this?

Use *Where* to ask about a place.

Where can he go?

Use *What* to ask about a thing.

What is his job?

Use *When* to ask about a time.

When is he at work?

B. Complete each question. Use *Who, What, Where,* or *When.*

1. Who drives the cab?
   Mr. Siwela drives the cab.
2. _____ is on his head?
   A cap is on his head.
3. _____ is the cab?
   The cab is at the flower shop.
4. _____ is the shop?
   The shop is on Main Street.

5. _____ wants a ride in the cab?
   Ms. Vega wants a ride.
6. _____ is in her hand?
   A plant is in her hand.
7. _____ is she ready to go?
   She is ready to go now.
8. _____ is her home?
   Her home is on Elm Street.

© NGSP & HB

Learn Key Vocabulary

Name _____

Geologists—Rock Scientists: Key Vocabulary

A. Study each word. Circle a number to rate how well you know it. Then complete the chart.

Rating Scale	1	2	3
	I have never seen this word before.	I am not sure of the word's meaning.	I know this word and can teach the word's meaning to someone else.

▲ **Scientists** called geologists can tell how old this **rock** is by **studying** its layers.

Key Words	Check Understanding	Deepen Understanding
1 learn (lurn) *verb* **Rating:** 1 2 3	To become a doctor, you must **learn** about the human body. **Yes** **No**	What do you like to learn about? _____ _____ _____ _____
2 rock (rok) *noun* **Rating:** 1 2 3	Most kinds of **rock** are soft. **Yes** **No**	Describe a kind of rock in your area. _____ _____ _____ _____
3 scientist (sī-yun-tist) *noun* **Rating:** 1 2 3	A **scientist** studies nature. **Yes** **No**	Name a kind of scientist. _____ _____ _____ _____

© NGSP & HB

Name _____

Scientists use tools to find clues in **rocks** about the past. ▶

Key Words	Check Understanding	Deepen Understanding
4 study (stuh-dē) *verb* **Rating:** 1 2 3	When you **study** science, you learn about plants and animals. **Yes** **No**	What will you study today? _____ _____ _____ _____
5 use (yūz) *verb* **Rating:** 1 2 3	Chefs **use** pots and pans. **Yes** **No**	What tools do farmers use? _____ _____ _____ _____

B. Use at least two of the Key Vocabulary words. Imagine you are a geologist. What would your day be like?

_____

_____

_____

© NGSP & HB

Writing Project

Name _____

Plan and Write

1. What worker will you interview? Name the worker's job. _____
2. What do you want to know? Make a list.

_____ _____

_____ _____

_____ _____

3. Choose a focus. Check three items.
4. Turn your ideas into questions. Write the questions. End each question with a **question mark.** Leave room for answers.

Q: What is _____

A: My name is _____

_____

Q: Where do _____

A: I work _____

_____

Q: What is _____

A: _____

_____

Q: What do you like _____

A: I like _____

_____

Q: _____

A: _____

_____

5. Study the questions. Interview a worker. Write your answers and get a photo or draw a picture of the person.

© NGSP & HB

Name _____

Check Your Work

Mark Your Changes

∧ **Add.**

≡ **Capitalize.**

▶ Capitalization and End Marks

Read the interview. Fix capital letters and end marks where they are needed. Mark your changes. Then write the sentences correctly.

Animal Doctor

Q: what is your name and what is your job

_____

A: my name is Martin Lee and I am an animal doctor

_____

Q: where do you work

_____

A: i work in an animal hospital on Park Street

_____

Q: what made you want to do this job

_____

A: i have always loved animals i lived on a farm when I was growing up

_____

_____

Q: what do you like best about your job

_____

A: my favorite thing is seeing animals get better my work makes people happy, too that's because pets are very important to people

_____

_____

_____

© NGSP & HB

Name _____

Mind Map

Use the mind map to show the different things that numbers can tell you. As you read the selections in this unit, add new ideas you learn about how numbers are used.

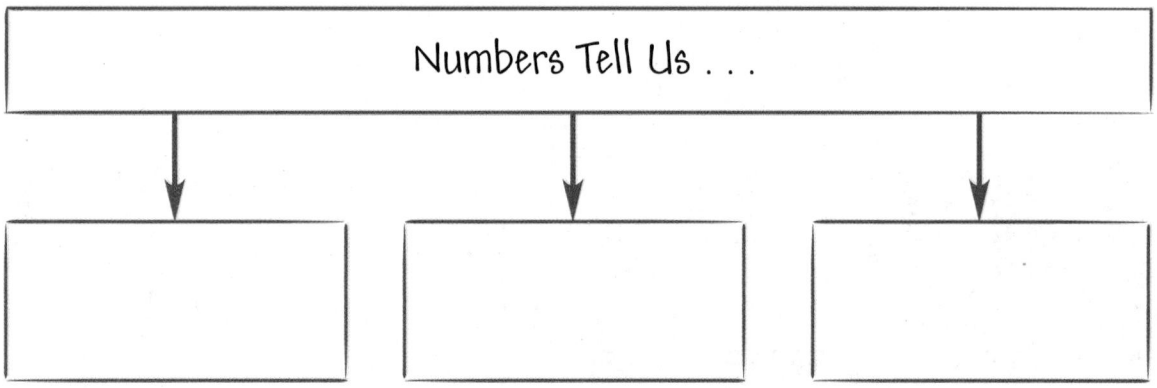

© NGSP & HB

Name _____

What Questions Do They Ask?

▶ **Language: Ask Questions**

▶ **Grammar: Questions with *Do* and *Does***

Complete each question. Then complete the answer.
Use *do* or *does*.

Questions with *Do* and *Does*

Use ***do*** with ***I***, ***you***, ***we***, and ***they***.
Do you have three caps?

Use ***does*** with ***he***, ***she***, and ***it***.
Does she need two bags?

1.

2.

3.

4.

© NGSP & HB

Name _____

Numbers Tell How Many

▶ **Vocabulary: Cardinal Numbers**

▶ **Language: Give Information**

A. Read the number words. Write the numbers.

1. four thousand, five hundred forty 4,540
2. nine hundred ninety-seven _____
3. three hundred ten thousand _____
4. two million, one hundred thousand _____
5. fifty-four thousand, one hundred one _____
6. eight hundred thirty-eight _____
7. five thousand, six hundred fourteen _____
8. seven hundred nineteen _____
9. thirty million, two hundred thousand _____
10. ten thousand, four hundred one _____

B. Complete the facts about this student's school. Use number words.

11. My school has three fields .
(3 fields)

12. My school _____ .
(12 classrooms)

13. My school _____
(24 computers)
_____ .

14. My school _____
(347 students)
_____ .

© NGSP & HB

Name _____

I Am Not Ready!

▶ Grammar: Negative Sentences

There are different ways to build negative sentences.

Add ***not*** after ***am, is,*** or ***are***.

He is ready. He is not ready.

Add ***do not*** or ***does not*** before other verbs.

He gets on the bus. He does not get on the bus.

A. Make each sentence a negative sentence. Use a verb and the word *not*.

1. I am ready for the game.

   I _____ ready for the game.

2. The bus is on time.

   The bus _____ on time.

3. We are on Bus 5.

   We _____ on Bus 5.

B. Make each sentence a negative sentence. Add *do not* or *does not*.

4. The bus driver leaves at 4:00.

   The bus driver _____ at 4:00.

5. She closes the doors.

   She _____ the doors.

6. The players go to the game.

   The players _____ to the game.

© NGSP & HB

 Name _____

First, Second, Third . . .

- **Vocabulary: Ordinal Numbers**
- **Language: Express Needs**

A. Look at the picture. In what order are the people?
Write words from the box to show the order.

first	second	third	fourth	fifth	sixth	seventh	eighth	ninth	tenth

B. Use the picture above to complete each sentence. Tell what the person needs.

mother	sneakers	bag	food	tag

1. The first person needs sneakers.
2. The fourth person needs a _____.
3. The sixth person needs a big _____.
4. The seventh person needs his _____.
5. The tenth person needs _____.

© NGSP & HB

Name _____

Identify Problem and Solution

▶ Sum It Up

Read the story. Complete the problem-and-solution chart. Use your chart to retell the story to a partner.

Friends to the Rescue

Morris opened his lunch bag as he talked to his friends. Suddenly, his face changed. He pulled out two small toy trucks.

"Oh, no," Morris groaned. "I picked up the wrong bag. This is what my mom bought for my little brother. I don't have anything to eat."

"You can have half of my peanut butter and jelly sandwich," said Pam.

"Here, take some of these. I can't eat all these grapes," said Jeff.

"I'll share my carton of juice with you," offered Jack.

"Thanks, everybody," Morris said. "What teamwork!"

Problem-and-Solution Chart

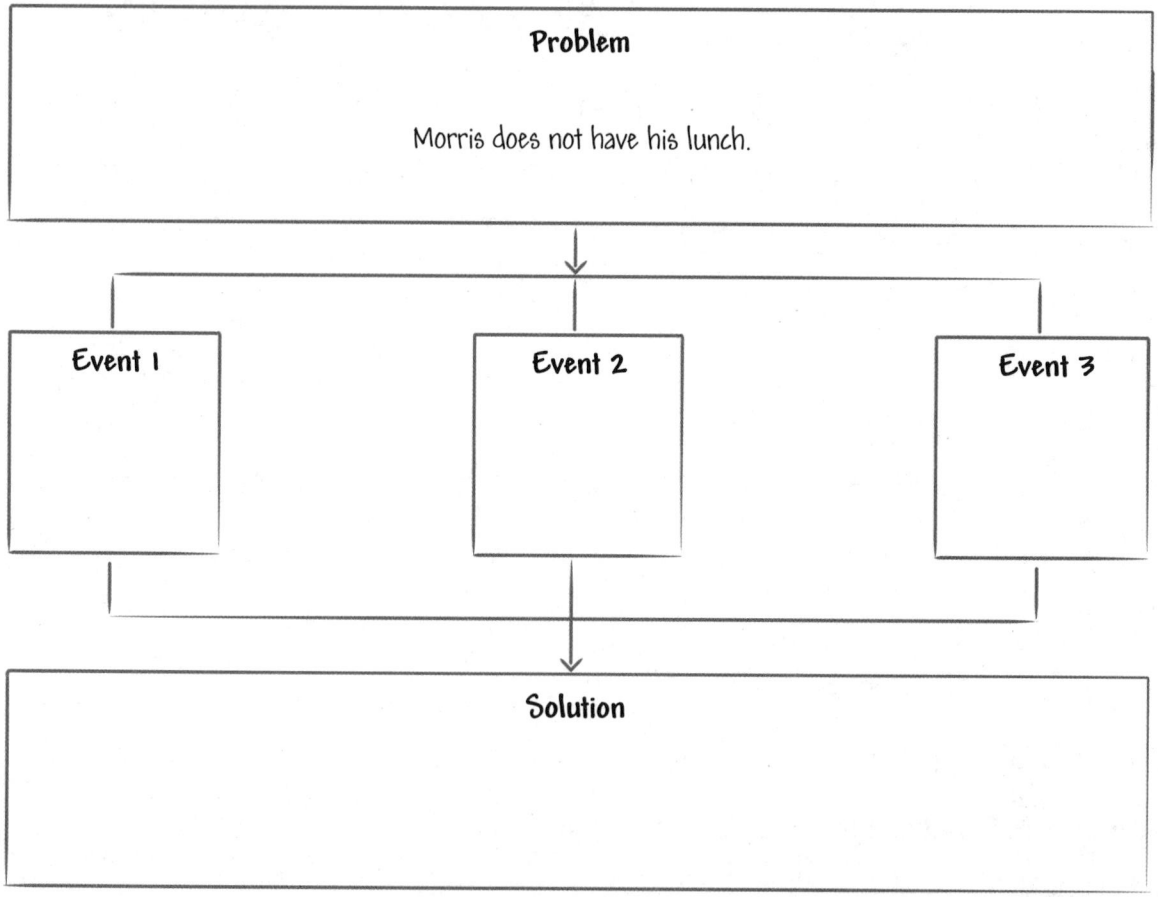

© NGSP & HB

Name _____

High Frequency Words, Part 1

A. Read each word. Then write it.

1. leave _____
2. two _____
3. out _____
4. three _____
5. all _____

B. Work with a partner. Follow the steps.

- Read aloud each new word in the box.
- Your partner writes the words.
- Have your partner read the words to you.
- Now you write the words on the lines below.
- Read the words to your partner.

6. _____
7. _____
8. _____
9. _____
10. _____

© NGSP & HB

Name _____

High Frequency Words, Part 2

A. Read each word. Then write it.

1. says _____
2. second _____
3. without _____
4. enough _____
5. more _____

B. Find the new words in the box. Write the words on the lines.

6. These 2 words begin with **s**.

says _____ _____

C. Work with a partner. Follow the steps.

- Read aloud each new word in the box.
- Your partner writes the words.
- Have your partner read the words to you.
- Now you write the words on the lines below.
- Read the words to your partner.

7. _____
8. _____
9. _____
10. _____
11. _____

© NGSP & HB

Name _____

Words with Digraphs

A. Name each picture. Write the name.

1. 

trash

2. 

_____

3. 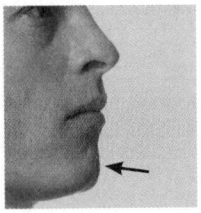

_____

4. 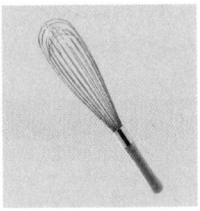

_____

5. 

_____

6. 

_____

7. 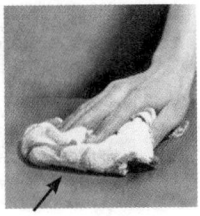

_____

8. 

_____

B. Now read the story. Circle the words that go in the chart. Write them in the chart. Write each word one time.

A Trip to the Shop

Dad and I go out to a shop. I think it sells great shells. We can bring some to Mom. I pick six shells and Dad pays cash. There is one more thing we want to do – find some fresh fish to eat. When we go home, Dad gives Mom the shells. Mom loves them and puts them on a shelf. What a great day!

Starts with *th*	Starts with *sh*
9. the	16. Shop
10. _____	17. _____
11. _____	18. _____
12. _____	
13. _____	
Ends with *ng*	**Ends with *sh***
14. _____	19. _____
15. _____	20. _____
	21. _____

© NGSP & HB

Name _____

Words with Blends and Digraphs

A. Name each picture. Write the name.

1. 

check

2. 

_____

3. 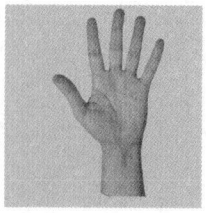

_____

4. 

_____

5. 

_____

6. 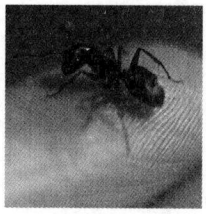

_____

B. Now read the story. Circle the words that go in the chart. Write them in the chart. Write each word one time.

Sal's Big Trunk

Sal has a big trunk. He fills it with things. Open the trunk and look in. You will see five clocks, sixteen red caps, a brush for a cat, and ten tops. You will see a chess set, a little lamp, a belt, twenty rocks, and bath stuff.

Do you like Sal's trunk? We can shut the trunk now.

Starts with *tr*	Ends with *mp*
7. trunk	11. _____
Starts with *cl*	**Ends with *lt***
8. _____	12. _____
Starts with *sh*	**Ends with *sh***
9. _____	13. _____
Starts with *ch*	**Ends with *th***
10. _____	14. _____

© NGSP & HB

Name _____

Words with Blends

A. Name each picture. Write the name.

1. 

spots

2. 

_____

3. 

_____

4. 

_____

5. 

_____

6. 

_____

7. 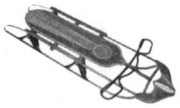

_____

8. 

_____

B. Now read the story. Circle the words that go in the chart. Write them in the chart. Write each word one time.

Pack for Camp

Jim packs his bag for camp. He needs enough stuff to last 5 days.

He packs:

- 1 tent and a mat to sleep on
- 2 swim trunks for his swim class
- a belt, 4 snacks, 10 socks, 1 brush, and more!

He can smash it all in the bag, but he can not lift the bag! Jim has to pack two bags for camp.

Starts with *st*	Ends with *st*
9. _____	13. _____
Starts with *tr*	**Ends with *nt***
10. _____	14. _____
Starts with *cl*	**Ends with *mp***
11. _____	15. Camp
Starts with *sn*	**Ends with *lt***
12. _____	16. _____

© NGSP & HB

Name _____

Build Reading Fluency

▶ Phrasing

A. When you read, pause between groups of words that go together.

Stan is in / a big rush. //
Stan has three minutes / to catch his plane. //

B. Listen to the story. When you hear a short pause, write a / . When you hear a long pause, write //.

Rush!

Stan is in a big rush. His plane leaves at 2:00 p.m. The clock says 1:57 p.m. Stan has three minutes to catch his plane. That is not very long! He jumps out of the cab and slams the door. Bang! He drops his bag. All of his things fall out of the bag. Then he drops one more thing—his ticket! A man helps Stan. The first thing he picks up is the bag. The second thing he picks up is the ticket. The man asks Stan, "When does your plane leave?"

Stan says, "I think it just left without me."

The man looks at Stan's ticket. He grins and tells Stan, "You have enough time. Your plane leaves tomorrow at two.

C. Now read the story to a partner. Read groups of words together. Pause when you see a /.

© NGSP & HB

Name _____

I Don't Want This Food!

▶ Contractions with *not*

A. When you make a contraction, you join two words together.

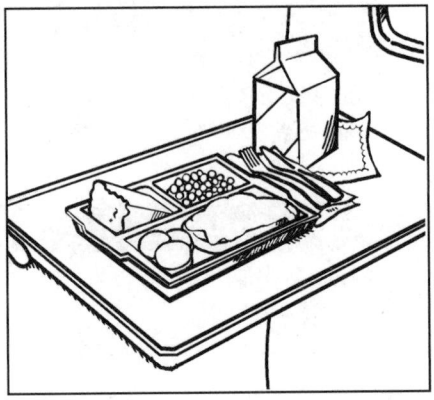

is + not = isn't	do + not = don't
are + not = aren't	does + not = doesn't

Use these contractions in negative sentences.

The food on the plane **isn't** very good.
The cookies **aren't** big.
The cake **doesn't** have nuts.
I **don't** want anything to eat.

B. Read each sentence. Change the underlined words to a contraction. Then complete the new sentence.

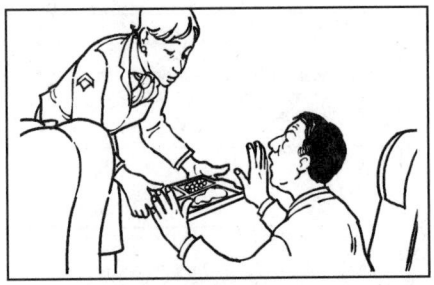

1. He is not happy.
   He ___isn't___ happy.

2. He does not like the food.
   He _____ like the food.

3. She does not eat the cake.
   She _____ eat the cake.

4. The cake is not sweet.
   The cake _____ sweet.

5. They do not want to eat.
   They _____ want to eat.

6. They are not hungry.
   They _____ hungry.

© NGSP & HB

Learn Key Vocabulary

Name _____

The Mighty Maya: Key Vocabulary

A. Study each word. Circle a number to rate how well you know it. Then complete the chart.

Rating Scale	1	2	3
	I have never seen this word before.	I am not sure of the word's meaning.	I know this word and can teach the word's meaning to someone else.

▲ This building was made **thousands** of years ago.

Key Words	Check Understanding	Deepen Understanding
❶ city (**si**-tē) *noun* **Rating:** 1 2 3	A **city** is very small with few people. **Yes** **No**	What city is close to you? _____ _____ _____ _____
❷ hundreds (**hun**-dridz) *noun* **Rating:** 1 2 3	An hour has **hundreds** of minutes. **Yes** **No**	Name a place where you can see hundreds of people. _____ _____ _____ _____
❸ population (pop-yū-**lā**-shun) *noun* **Rating:** 1 2 3	**Population** tells how many people live in one area. **Yes** **No**	Name a state with a big population. _____ _____ _____ _____

© NGSP & HB

Key Vocabulary, continued

Name _____

These **two** men are Mayan. ▶

Key Words	Check Understanding	Deepen Understanding
❹ thousands (**thou**-zundz) *noun* **Rating:** 1 2 3	Texas has **thousands** of people. **Yes** **No**	Name a number in the thousands. _____ _____ _____ _____
❺ two (tū) *adjective* **Rating:** 1 2 3	A bike has **two** wheels. **Yes** **No**	Name two different holidays. _____ _____ _____ _____

B. Use at least two of the Key Vocabulary words. Describe the population of your class. Is it large or small?

_____

_____

_____

© NGSP & HB

Writing Project

Name _____

Plan and Write

1. What country will you research? _____
2. What do you want to know? Make a list.

_____ _____

_____ _____

_____ _____

3. Choose your focus. Check three items.
4. Turn your list into questions. Write the questions. Research in books or on the Internet to find the answers to your questions. Write your answers. Draw a map of your country in the box at the top.

Facts About _____

- How large is _____

  The country of _____

  is _____

- What is the _____

  _____

  _____

  _____

- What is _____

  _____

  _____

  _____

A map of _____

© NGSP & HB

Name _____

Check Your Work

Mark Your Changes

∧ **Add.**

≡ **Capitalize.**

▶ Capitalization and End Marks

Read the fact sheet. Fix capital letters and add end punctuation as needed. Mark your changes. Then write the questions and answers correctly.

Facts About Mexico

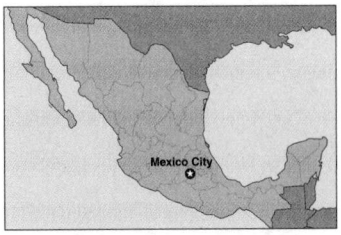

A map of Mexico

- How large is mexico

_____

mexico is about 742,485 square miles.

_____

- What is the population of mexico?

_____

The population of Mexico is 108,700,891.

_____

- What is the longest river in mexico

_____

The rio grande is the longest river in Mexico.

_____

- What is the population of the capital city of mexico

_____

The capital city is Mexico city. The population of mexico city is 19,013,000.

_____

© NGSP & HB

Name _____

Mind Map

Use the mind map to show how to find out about your town or city. As you read the selections in this unit, add new ideas for ways to learn about a city.

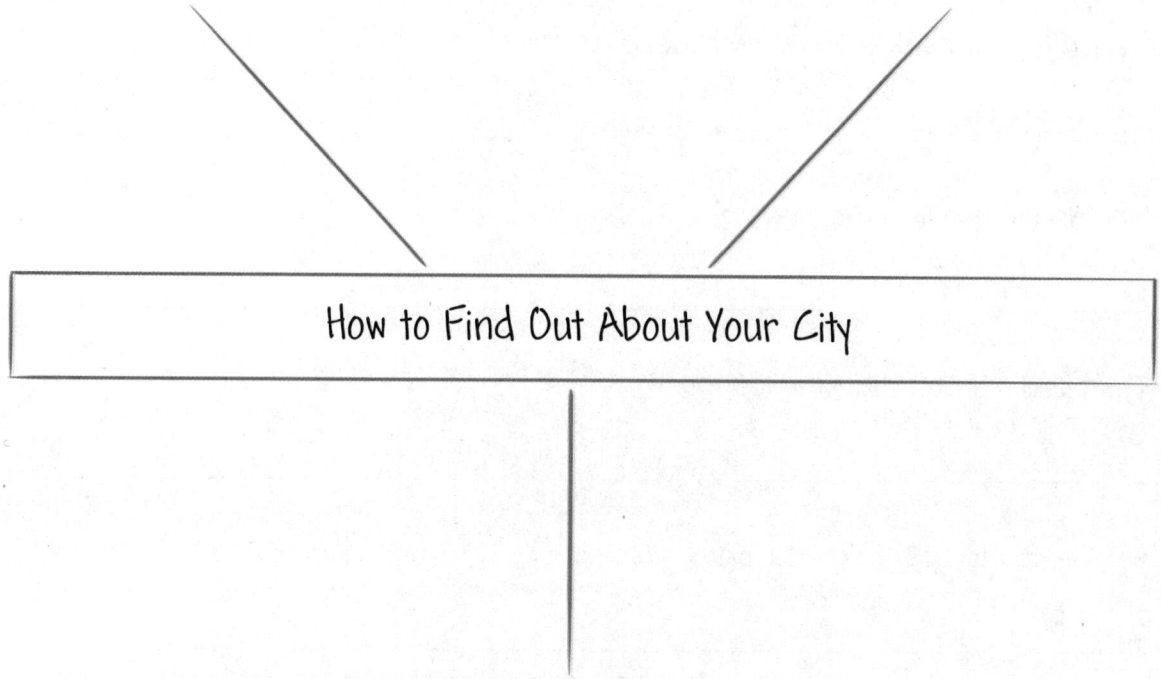

© NGSP & HB

Language Development

Name _____

Where Is It?

▶ **Language: Ask For and Give Information**

▶ **Vocabulary: Location Words**

Location Words

in
on
by, near
above, over
below, under
next to, beside
between
down
behind, in back of

A. Study the places.

B. Complete each sentence. Tell where the places are. Use location words.

1. The pet shop is ___on___ the corner.
2. You can get dog food _____ the pet shop.
3. The toy store is _____ the café.
4. The toy store is _____ the music store and the market.
5. You go _____ the stairs to get from the market to the bakery.
6. The market is _____ the bakery.
7. The café is _____ the bakery.
8. There are two plants _____ the café.
9. There is someone _____ the door to the bakery.
10. The theater is _____ the pet shop.

© NGSP & HB

Name _____

Things in the Neighborhood

- **Vocabulary: Neighborhood**
- **Language: Ask For and Give Information**

A. Name each place. Then name something you see there. Use words from the box.

intersection	post office	bus station	store	bus	parking lot	mailbox	stop sign

1. 

bus station

2. 

_____

3. 

_____

4. 

_____

B. Answer each question. Use a complete sentence.

5. What happens at the bus station?

People wait for the bus.

6. What happens at the intersection?

_____

7. What happens at the store?

_____

8. What happens at the post office?

_____

© NGSP & HB

Name _____

On My Street

▶ Grammar: Regular Past Tense Verbs

A verb changes to show the past tense.

She **cooks** the food.

She **cooked** the food.

Look at each picture. Read the sentence. Circle the correct verb.

1. 

They **play / played** soccer.

2. 

She **parks / parked** her car.

3. 

He **opens / opened** the bag of chips.

4. 

She **adds / added** flowers to the garden.

5. 

He **cleans / cleaned** the car.

6. 

They **help / helped** win the game.

© NGSP & HB

Name _____

We Visited the Zoo

▶ Regular Past Tense Verbs

You can add *–ed* to many verbs to tell about things that happened in the past.

We **wanted** to go to the city zoo.

I **asked** Mom to take us there.

Complete each sentence. Add the past tense of the verb in dark type.

1. We walked around the zoo. **(walk)**
2. Sam _____ the young lions. **(watch)**
3. They _____ so big! **(look)**
4. Tara _____ away from them! **(stay)**
5. I _____ to see the monkeys. **(ask)**

6. They _____ all around. **(jump)**
7. One monkey _____ a ball. **(toss)**
8. We _____ to them yell! **(listen)**
9. Mom _____ . **(laugh)**
10. We all _____ our visit. **(enjoy)**

© NGSP & HB

 Name _____

Identify Details

▶ Sum It Up

A. Read what Sergio did in his neighborhood. Make a detail chart to show what he did and when he did it. The first row in the chart has been filled in for you.

Sergio's Busy Week

Sergio has many nice neighbors. He spent a lot of time this week helping them after school. On Monday, Sergio shopped for dog treats. Then he walked Mrs. Perez's dog. On Tuesday, he mowed the grass for Mr. Mendez. He read the paper to Mr. Mendez, too. On Wednesday, Sergio carried groceries for Mrs. Gold. Then he stacked groceries on her kitchen shelves. On Thursday, Sergio watched Mrs. Lee's twin boys. On Friday, Sergio played baseball after school. All the neighbors went to the game and cheered for him!

Detail Chart

Day	Events
Monday	shopped for dog treats, walked dog

B. Imagine that you are one of Sergio's neighbors. Write a thank-you note to thank him for helping you.

Dear Sergio,

Thank you for _____

_____

_____

Your neighbor,

_____

© NGSP & HB

Name _____

High Frequency Words, Part 1

A. Read each word. Then write it.

1. city _____
2. above _____
3. by _____
4. sometimes _____
5. her _____

B. Read each sentence. Find the new words in the box. Write the words on the lines.

6. These 2 words end with **y**.

   city _____ _____

7. These 2 words are location words.

   _____ _____

8. This word rhymes with **my**.

   _____

9. This word has 2 smaller words in it.

   _____

10. This word has **er**.

    _____

© NGSP & HB

Name _____

High Frequency Words, Part 2

A. Read each word. Then write it.

1. come _____
2. animals _____
3. people _____
4. down _____
5. under _____

B. Read each sentence. Find the new words in the box. Write the words on the lines.

6. This word starts with **c**.

   come

7. These 2 words name living things.

   _____ _____

8. These 2 words are location words.

   _____ _____

9. These 2 words end with **e**.

   _____ _____

10. This word has **er**.

    _____

© NGSP & HB

Name _____

Words with Long and Short Vowels

A. Name each picture. Read the two words. Circle the word that names the picture.

1. 

face / fact

2. 

hi / hill

3. 

be / bell

4. 

wet / we

B. Now read the story. Circle the words with long *e*. Then circle the words with short *e*. Write them in the chart. Write each word one time.

We Like to Swim!

We like to swim. But I do not like to get wet! The pool is near my home. I walk there with Kim. She is my friend. We can be in the water until the bell rings. Then we have to get out. As we wait, I get dry. When they let us back in the pool, I get wet again! I like to swim so much that I do not mind if I get wet. Kim bet me I would like swimming more if I could stay dry, but I cannot do that! She is funny.

Words with long e	Words with short e
5. we	9. get
6. _____	10. _____
7. _____	11. _____
8. _____	12. _____
	13. _____
	14. _____
	15. _____

© NGSP & HB

Name _____

Words with Long and Short Vowels

A. Name each picture. Read the two words. Circle the word that names the picture.

1. 

he / hen

2. 

he / help

3. 

hi / hit

4. 

be / bell

B. Now read the story. Circle the words with long *e*. Then circle the words with short *e*. Write them in the chart. Write each word one time.

At Home in the City

I like my home in the city. On Saturdays, Sal and I help at the library. He sits at the desk. I show the kids good books. Then I let them look around without me. At 12:00, we are done. Sometimes we stop for lunch. Then we go home. We walk down Grand Road. The city is so great! We can be home in two minutes.

Words with long *e*	Words with short *e*
5. he	9. help
6. _____	10. _____
7. _____	11. _____
8. _____	12. _____
	13. _____

© NGSP & HB

Name _____

Multisyllabic Words

A. Read each word. Write how many syllables it has.

1. 
pool
1

2. 
nickel
_____

3. 
moon
_____

4. 
garden
_____

5. 
basket
_____

6. 
napkin
_____

7. 
screw
_____

8. 
broom
_____

B. Now read the story. Circle the words with two syllables. Write each word in the chart. Then write the syllables.

Hunting a Pumpkin

We went to find a pumpkin at the farm. We wanted the biggest one in the field. My sister helped me look. We saw a lot of pumpkins. We also saw a snake! My mom was calling to us. The farmer told us to look in the far corner of the field. There we saw the biggest pumpkin in the whole field! Next to it was a small one. We could not carry the big pumpkin, so we picked the small one.

Word	Syllable	
9. hunting	hunt	ing
10.		
11.		
12.		
13.		
14.		
15.		
16.		
17.		
18.		

© NGSP & HB

Name _____

Multisyllabic Words

A. Read each word. Write how many syllables it has.

1. 

basket

2 _____

2. 

pumpkin

_____

3. 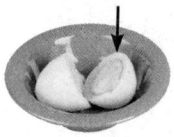

egg

_____

4. 

muffin

_____

5. 

stamp

_____

6. 

plate

_____

7. 

napkin

_____

8. 

bench

_____

B. Now read the story. Circle the words with two syllables. Write each word in the chart. Then write the syllables.

A Picnic in the Park

Jan and Chun go on a picnic. Jan packs lunch in a basket. Chun grabs a blanket. Then they put on their helmets and hop on their bikes. They ride through a tunnel, then up to Elm Road. They watch out for traffic. At the park, they see lots of children. Chun puts the blanket on the grass, and they sit down. "Let's eat," Jan says. "Do you want a sandwich?"

Word	Syllable	
9. picnic	pic	nic
10.		
11.		
12.		
13.		
14.		
15.		
16.		

© NGSP & HB

Name _____

Build Reading Fluency

▶ Expression

A. Some sentences tell something. Other sentences show strong feeling.

This sentence tells something. It ends with a period.

Jo works at the City Animal Hospital .

This sentence shows a strong feeling.
It ends with an exclamation mark.

He is so soft !

B. Listen to the different kinds of sentences.

Meet Jo

Jo works at the City Animal Hospital. I asked her to tell me about what she does at her job.

I have a great job. I love to help the animals. Look. This cat got hit by traffic. It is so sad when that happens. I had to make her a special bed. She has to lie down a lot.

This is Samson. Samson has a bad rash. He has this thing around his neck so he can't bite the skin under it. Sometimes we play catch. He needs to run a lot. He likes to run down the hill to the park. We rest under the trees. I like to look at the sky above us as Samson sleeps.

This rabbit is Velvet. I like to brush him. He is so soft! Velvet had to get his shots. He needs to rest for a day or two. Then he will go home.

So, that is my job. I help hundreds of animals. It is great to see them get well. I miss them when people come to take them home.

C. Now read the sentences to a partner. See how your reading improves!

© NGSP & HB

Name _____

They're from My Neighborhood

▶ Pronoun-Verb Contractions

A. You can put a pronoun and a verb together to form a contraction.

I + am = I'm	**I'm** on the sidewalk.
you + are = you're	**You're** slow.
he + is = he's she + is = she's it + is = it's	**It's** a sunny day.
we + are = we're	**We're** glad to be together.
they + are = they're	**They're** in the park.

B. Combine the words in dark type to make a contraction. Use the contraction to complete the sentence.

1. Sam and Kim are Mia's friends. They're her neighbors.
   (They are)
2. Mia walks the dogs for Sam and Kim. _____ happy to do it.
   (She is)
3. One dog stops to rest. _____ a small dog.
   (He is)
4. Mia laughs at the dog. "_____ slow, Biff."
   (You are)
5. "You can rest, Biff. _____ not in a hurry."
   (We are)
6. Mia waits for Biff. _____ nice to all the dogs.
   (She is)
7. People look at the dogs. _____ surprised to see so many!
   (They are)
8. Soon the walk is over. _____ time to eat.
   (It is)

© NGSP & HB

Learn Key Vocabulary

Name _____

San Francisco: Key Vocabulary

A. Study each word. Circle a number to rate how well you know it. Then complete the chart.

Rating Scale	1	2	3
	I have never seen this word before.	I am not sure of the word's meaning.	I know this word and can teach the word's meaning to someone else.

▲ The city of San Francisco has many tall **buildings**.

Key Words	Check Understanding	Deepen Understanding
1 buildings (**bil**-dings) *noun* **Rating:** 1 2 3	Houses are **buildings**. **Yes** **No**	What makes buildings look good? _____ _____ _____ _____
2 live (**liv**) *verb* **Rating:** 1 2 3	Many people **live** in cities. **Yes** **No**	Where would you like to live? _____ _____ _____ _____
3 neighborhood (**nā**-bor-hood) *noun* **Rating:** 1 2 3	A **neighborhood** is made up of homes and shops. **Yes** **No**	Describe your neighborhood. _____ _____ _____ _____

© NGSP & HB

Key Vocabulary, continued

Name _____

San Francisco was once a small **town** with only a few **buildings** like this one. ▶

Key Words	Check Understanding	Deepen Understanding
4 store (stor) *noun* **Rating:** 1 2 3	You can buy things at a **store**. **Yes** **No**	Describe a store near you. _____ _____ _____ _____
5 town (toun) *noun* **Rating:** 1 2 3	A **town** and a city are the same size. **Yes** **No**	Tell about a town that you have visited. _____ _____ _____ _____

B. Use at least two of the Key Vocabulary words. Tell what makes your neighborhood special.

_____

_____

_____

© NGSP & HB

Writing Project

Name _____

Plan and Write

1. Think about things you did last week. Complete the chart.

Day	Events	Place
Monday		
Tuesday		
Wednesday		
Thursday		
Friday		
Saturday		
Sunday		

2. Use your notes to write a journal page. Use past tense verbs.

Last Monday, I _____

On Tuesday, _____

On Wednesday, _____

On Thursday, _____

On Friday, _____

On Saturday, _____

On Sunday, _____

© NGSP & HB

Name _____

Check Your Work

Mark Your Changes

∧ **Add.**

≡ **Capitalize.**

▶ Capitalization and End Marks

Read this journal page. Fix capital letters and add end punctuation as needed. Mark your changes. Then write each sentence correctly.

Last monday, i played baseball in the park

_____

On tuesday, I looked for books in the library

_____

On wednesday, i shopped at the mall

_____

On Thursday, i went to dinner in a restaurant

_____

On friday, I visited my friend at her house

_____

On saturday, I cleaned my bedroom

_____

On sunday, i cooked breakfast in my kitchen

_____

© NGSP & HB

Name _____

Mind Map

Use the mind map to show what you know about family life. As you read the selections in this unit, add new ideas you learn about the people, places, and events that are part of family life.

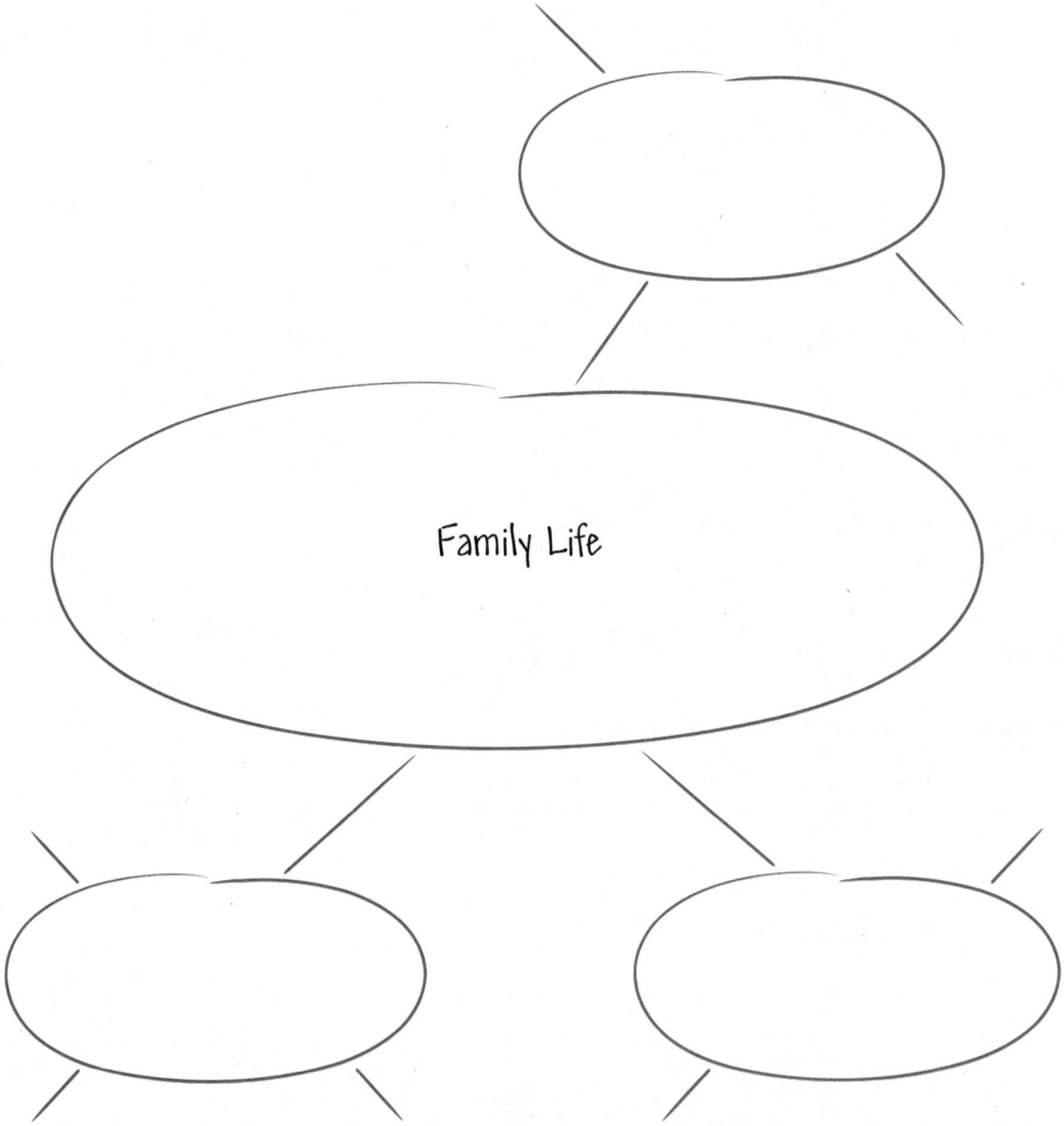

© NGSP & HB

Name _____

Meet Lin's Family

▶ **Language: Give Information**

▶ **Vocabulary: Family**

Family Words

grandfather	**brother**
grandmother	**sister**
father	**uncle**
mother	**aunt**

A. Use family words to tell about Lin's family tree. Then answer the question below.

Lin's Family Tree

B. How many people are in Lin's family? _____ of them together make up Lin's family tree.

© NGSP & HB

Name _____

I Have a Great Family

▶ Grammar: Present Tense Verbs: *Have* and *Has*

Use *have* with *I*, *you*, *we*, and *they*. Use *has* with *he*, *she*, or *it*.

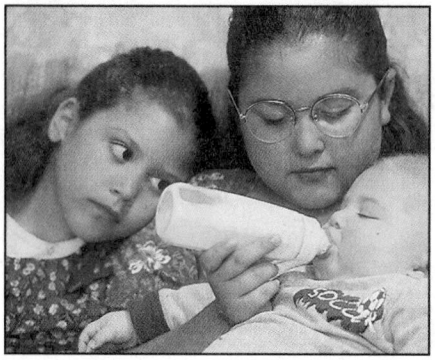

Hi. I'm Rita. I **have** a sister. We **have** a new brother. He **has** a room. It **has** toys in it.

Complete each sentence. Use *have* or *has*.

1. 

"I ___have___ an aunt."

"She _____ a dog."

2. 

"We _____ a small house."

"The house _____ trees around it."

3. 

He _____ a sister.

They _____ fun together.

4. 

He _____ an uncle.

His uncle _____ a big bike.

© NGSP & HB

Name _____

What Is in Each Room?

- **Vocabulary: Household Objects**
- **Language: Ask and Answer Questions**

A. Name the things in each room. Use words from the box.

bathtub	**bed**	**lamp**	**oven**
couch	**dresser**	**sink**	**shower**
stove	**rug**	**refrigerator**	**door**

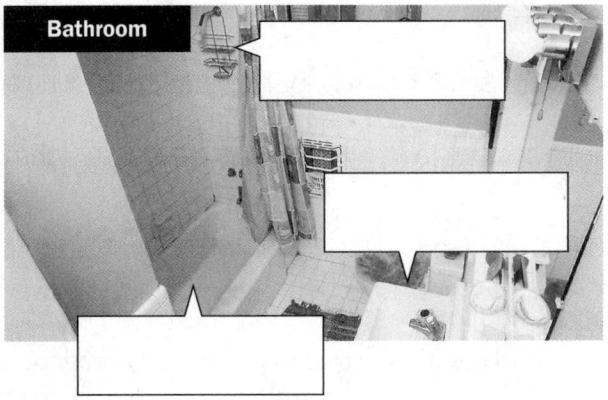

B. Answer each question. Use a complete sentence.

1. Where is the couch? The couch is in the living room.
2. Where is the dresser? _____
3. Where is the oven? _____

C. Write two questions. Ask about two things in the rooms above.

4. _____
5. _____

© NGSP & HB

Name _____

Identify Details that Support a Main Idea

▶ Sum It Up

Read the following article. Read the main idea. Write the important ideas in the Main Idea Diagram.

Chinese Family Traditions

Families that lived a long time ago in China had many traditions. Grandparents lived with one of their children and helped take care of the grandchildren. Then as the grandparents got older, their children and grandchildren took care of them. Babies were often named after family members from older generations. Holidays such as the Chinese New Year were celebrated with family members. Younger people showed respect to older people. The older people gave gifts to the youngsters. When it was time to marry, the parents or grandparents chose a husband or wife for their child. The Chinese believed that their traditions made strong families.

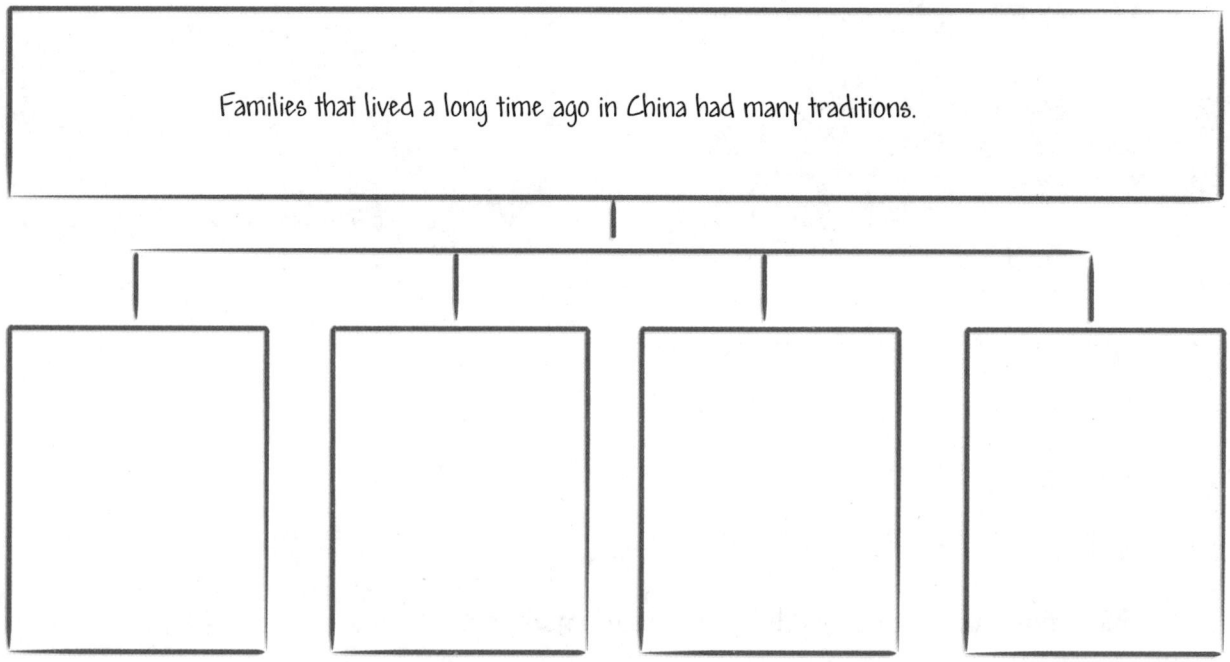

© NGSP & HB

Name _____

High Frequency Words, Part 1

A. Read each word. Then write it.

1. family _____
2. together _____
3. other _____
4. really _____
5. father _____

B. Read the clue. Write the word in the chart. Then write the word again in the sentence.

What to Look For	Word	Sentence
6. begins with **fam**	f a m i l y	My family loves games.
7. begins with **to**	___ ___ ___ ___ ___ ___ ___ ___	We like to be _____ .
8. begins with **o**	___ ___ ___ ___ ___	We do _____ things, too.
9. begins with **r**	___ ___ ___ ___ ___ ___	We have a _____ big family.
10. means "dad"	___ ___ ___ ___ ___ ___	My _____ is an artist.

© NGSP & HB

Name _____

High Frequency Words, Part 2

A. Read each word. Then write it.

1. mother _____
2. our _____
3. watch _____
4. eyes _____
5. head _____

B. Read the clue. Write the word in the chart. Then write the word again in the sentence.

What to Look For	Word	Sentence
6. means "mom"	m o t h e r	My mother is a writer.
7. has 3 letters	___ ___ ___	Friday is _____ game night.
8. ends with **tch**	___ ___ ___ ___ ___	Sometimes we _____ TV.
9. has **yes** in it	___ ___ ___ ___	I use my _____ to do puzzles.
10. rhymes with **bed**	___ ___ ___ ___	I think with my _____ .

© NGSP & HB

Name _____

Words with Long Vowels: *a_e, o_e*

A. Name each picture. Write the name.

1. 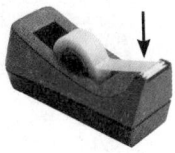

tape

2. 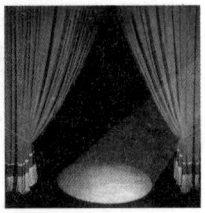

_____

3. 

_____

4. 

_____

5. 

_____

6. 

_____

7. 

_____

8. 

_____

B. Now read the story. Circle the words with long *a* or long *o*. Write them in the chart. Write each word one time.

Trouble at the Lake

Our home is close to a lake. The lake is big. Sometimes it has big waves.

One day I take a ride and get to the lake. I gaze out. Those waves are big! I see a boy in trouble. A man comes by and spots the boy. He jumps into the water and swims out with big strokes. I shut my eyes and hope he can save the boy. And he does!

I spoke to the man. "That was very brave!" I said.

9. Lake	15. _____
10. _____	16. _____
11. _____	17. _____
12. _____	18. _____
13. _____	19. _____
14. _____	20. _____

© NGSP & HB

Name _____

Words with Long Vowels

A. Name each picture. Write the name.

1. 

cape

2. 

_____

3. 

_____

4. 

_____

5. 

_____

6. 

_____

7. 

_____

8. 

_____

B. Now read the story. Circle the words with long *a, i, o,* or *u*. Write them in the chart. Write each word one time.

Fun with Bill

My brother Bill drives a truck all around the state. When he is home, he makes life fun.

Once he put together kites for all the kids in the family. Bill had to use long, thin tubes for the frames. The wings were cloth from a torn robe. "The kites are cute," he said, "but I hope we can get them up in the air!"

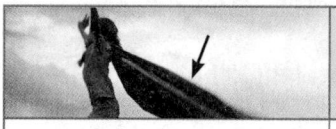	
9. _____	15. _____
10. _____	16. _____
11. _____	17. _____

12. drives	18. _____
13. _____	19. _____
14. _____	20. _____

© NGSP & HB

Name _____

Words with Short and Long Vowels

A. Name each picture. Read the two words. Circle the word that names the picture.

1. 

(cap) / cape

2. 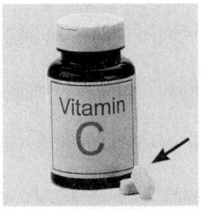

pill / pile

3. 

kit / kite

4. 

tub / tube

5. 

rob / robe

6. 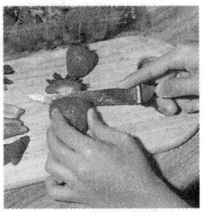

cut / cute

7. 

rod / rode

8. 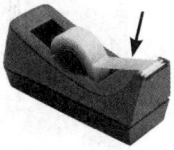

tap / tape

B. Now read the story. Circle the words with long *o* or long *i*. Underline the words with short *o* or short *i*. Write them in the chart. Write each word one time.

A Busy (Home)

We are really busy. Here is what a day is like. Mom drives to the pet shop. She must be there by three. The shop closes at three. Then Mom stops to get us snacks to eat. Dad helps me fix my bike, and then we scrub the stove. Pam has to watch the baby next door. At the end of the day, we like to sit down and rest. That is when we can all be together again.

9. Home	15. _____
10. _____	16. _____
11. _____	17. _____
	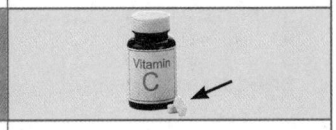
12. _____	18. _____
13. _____	19. _____
14. _____	20. _____

© NGSP & HB

Name _____

Plurals

A. Name each picture. Read the two words. Circle the word that names the picture.

1. 
boy / boys

2. 
state / states

3. 
pin / pins

4. 
duck / ducks

5. 
stripe / stripes

6. 
pear / pears

7. 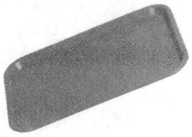
tray / trays

8. 
star / stars

B. Now read the story. Circle the words that name more than one thing. Write them in the chart. Write each word one time.

Parades in the City

Our city has many parades for kids. The parades are a lot of fun. Girls and boys pass by in bands. They play drums and trumpets and other things. Girls do tricks with batons. We see costumes with a lot of colors. We see many pets, too. Boys and girls pass by with their dogs, cats, and snakes. Parents stand on the sidewalk and clap. They like to see the kids.

Plurals	
9. parades	18. _____
10. _____	19. _____
11. _____	20. _____
12. _____	21. _____
13. _____	22. _____
14. _____	23. _____
15. _____	24. _____
16. _____	25. _____
17. _____	

© NGSP & HB

Name _____

Build Reading Fluency

▶ Phrasing

A. When you read, pause between groups of words that go together.

In Nicaragua, / my family made / big puppets to sell. //
We made the arms / from long tubes. //

B. Listen to the story. When you hear a short pause, write a / . When you hear a long pause, write //.

Example: In Nicaragua, / my family made / big puppets to sell.//

When We Came to Wisconsin

Hi. My name is Pablo Soto. My mother's name is Sandra. We are from Nicaragua.

In Nicaragua, our family made big puppets to sell. The name of one puppet that we made is *La Gigantona*. We made the head of this puppet with paper and paste. We made the eyes of the puppet really big, with long, thick lashes. We made the arms from long tubes. They swing from side to side. We put a white robe, a cute hat, and other things on the puppet. People like to watch this big puppet in parades.

C. Now read the story to a partner. Use the marks you made to read groups of words together.

© NGSP & HB

Name _____

New Neighbors

▶ Plural Nouns

A. A noun names a person, place, or thing.

A singular noun names one thing.

box

A plural noun names more than one thing.

boxes

Study these rules for forming plurals.

To make most nouns plural, just add **-s**.	boy boys	girl girls	book books
If the noun ends in **x, ch, sh, s,** or **z,** add **-es**.	box boxes	dish dishes	glass glasses
Some nouns change in different ways.	man men	woman women	child children

B. Complete each sentence. Use the plural form of the word in dark type.

1. Two ___women___ bring food.
   (woman)
2. There are many _____ to unpack.
   (box)

3. Mrs. Lee finds the _____ .
   (dish)
4. Then she finds the _____ .
   (cup)

5. They eat their _____ .
   (lunch)
6. Mrs. Lee has two new _____ .
   (friend)

© NGSP & HB

Learn Key Vocabulary

Name _____

The Family Reunion: Key Vocabulary

A. Study each word. Circle a number to rate how well you know it. Then complete the chart.

Rating Scale	1	2	3
	I have never seen this word before.	I am not sure of the word's meaning.	I know this word and can teach the word's meaning to someone else.

▲ This **family** is **together** at a party.

Key Words	Check Understanding	Deepen Understanding
1 cousins (**ku**-zinz) *noun* **Rating:** 1 2 3	My **cousins** are my mother's sisters. **Yes** **No**	How are cousins related to each other? _____ _____ _____ _____
2 family (**fa**-mu-lē) *noun* **Rating:** 1 2 3	A **family** can be big or small. **Yes** **No**	Name at least two people in your family. _____ _____ _____ _____
3 grandchildren (**grand**-chil-drun) *noun* **Rating:** 1 2 3	Grandparents can have many **grandchildren**. **Yes** **No**	Tell about the grandchildren in your family. _____ _____ _____ _____

© NGSP & HB

Name _____

These **parents** like to play music with their children. ▶

Key Words	Check Understanding	Deepen Understanding
❹ parents (pair-ents) *noun* **Rating:** 1 2 3	Your brother and sister are your **parents**. **Yes** **No**	Name something parents do for children. _____ _____ _____ _____
❺ together (tu-ge-thur) *adverb* **Rating:** 1 2 3	Children often play **together**. **Yes** **No**	What do you and your family do together? _____ _____ _____ _____

B. Use at least two of the Key Vocabulary words. Explain why it is important for family and friends to be together.

_____

_____

_____

© NGSP & HB

Writing Project

Name _____

Plan and Write

1. Choose two people to write about. Write their names in the first column. Then fill in the chart.

Who?	What the Person Likes	What the Person Does	Where	Something Special About the Person

2. Write a title and your name.

_____

by _____

3. Write 3 complete sentences about each person. Tell
   - what the person **likes**
   - what the person **has** and **where** it is
   - **something special** about the person

My _____ likes _____ .

_____ has _____ .

_____ is _____ .

© NGSP & HB

Name _____

Check Your Work

Mark Your Changes

∧ **Add.**

▶ Plurals and Details

Read the descriptions. Fix plural nouns as needed. Mark your changes. Then write the sentences correctly.

My Family

by Sara Thomas

Uncle Jackson likes trucks. He has two 1969 truck in his garage. He fixes broken car and truck.

_____

_____

_____

My sister Ramona likes playing in the park. She has a collection of toy car. Ramona can whistle.

_____

_____

_____

My brother Stuart likes to cook. He has his own pots and pan. He is a cook.

_____

_____

_____

My cousins like to play guitar. They have instrument. They know many song.

_____

_____

_____

© NGSP & HB

Name _____

Mind Map

Use the mind map to show what you know about the rain forest. As you read the selections in this unit, add new ideas you learn about the plants, animals, and landforms of the rain forest.

Pack Your Bags — for the Rain Forest!

Plants	Animals	Landforms	What to Pack

© NGSP & HB

Name _____

Give Commands

▶ Language: Give and Carry Out Commands

Commands
A **command** tells you what to do or what not to do.
Pack your bags.
Don't forget.

A. Study the commands.

Wear a jacket.	**Get some warm clothes.**	**Find a seat.**
Grab a camera.	**Ride the bus.**	**Pack your bag.**
Enjoy the trip!	**Take some gloves.**	**Step on the bus.**
Dress for snow.	**Don't forget a hat.**	**Take some film.**

B. Write two commands for each picture. Use commands from the box.

1. 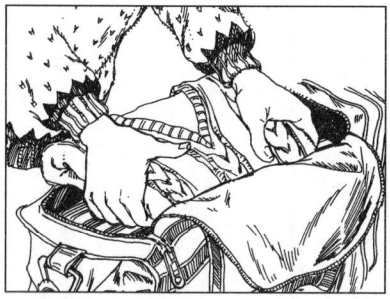

Get some warm clothes.

Pack your bag.

_____

2. 

_____

_____

_____

3. 

_____

_____

_____

4. 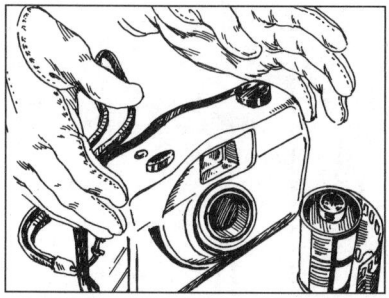

_____

_____

_____

5. 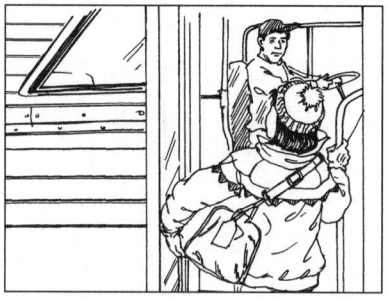

_____

_____

_____

6. 

_____

_____

_____

© NGSP & HB

Language Development

Name _____

What Do You See?

▶ **Vocabulary: Landforms and Transportation**

▶ **Language: Describe Places**

A. Name the places and things in the picture. Use words from the box.

ocean	forest	sailboat	airplane	beach	island

small	tall	hot	dry	fast

B. Complete each sentence. Describe the picture above. Use adjectives from the box.

1. The island has a forest with _____tall_____ trees.
2. A _____ airplane flies over the island.
3. A _____ sailboat sails on the ocean.
4. The _____ sun shines on the beach.
5. It makes the sand hot and _____ .

© NGSP & HB

Name _____

What Do They Wear?

- **Vocabulary: Weather and Clothing**
- **Language: Give Information**

A. Name the things to wear. Use words from the box.

sneaker	glove	scarf	bathing suit	sandal	parka

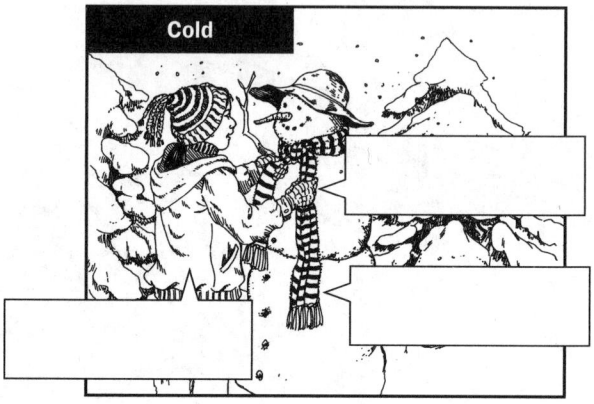

B. What is the weather like? Tell Brandon and Rachel what clothing to pack.

1. It is _____sunny_____ and _____warm_____ at the beach.
2. Take a _____ so you can swim.
3. Pack some _____ to wear on your feet.
4. Wear your _____ when it is really hot.
5. It is _____ in the mountains.
6. Take a warm coat or _____ .
7. Pack _____ to keep your hands warm.
8. Wear a _____ around your neck.

© NGSP & HB

 Name _____

Yes, You Can!

▶ Grammar: Use the Verb *Can*

Use *can* before another verb to tell what people are able to do.

can + sail = can sail

My father **can sail** a boat.

He **can take** my sister to an island.

She **can visit** her friends there.

Never add -s to *can*.

Complete each sentence. Tell what the people in each picture can do. Use *can* and a word from the box.

work	wear	see	hike	ski	play	plant	swim

winter

spring

summer

fall

1. In the winter, he can ski in the mountains.
2. In the winter, he _____ in the snow.
3. In the spring, she _____ in the garden.
4. In the spring, she _____ flowers.
5. In the summer, he _____ in the pool.
6. In the summer, he _____ a bathing suit.
7. In the fall, they _____ pretty trees.
8. In the fall, they _____ in the park.

© NGSP & HB

 Name _____

Classify Information

▶ Sum It Up

A. Think of a place you would like to explore. Write the name in the middle of the concept map below. Then write what you can see there, what the weather is like, and what you would wear.

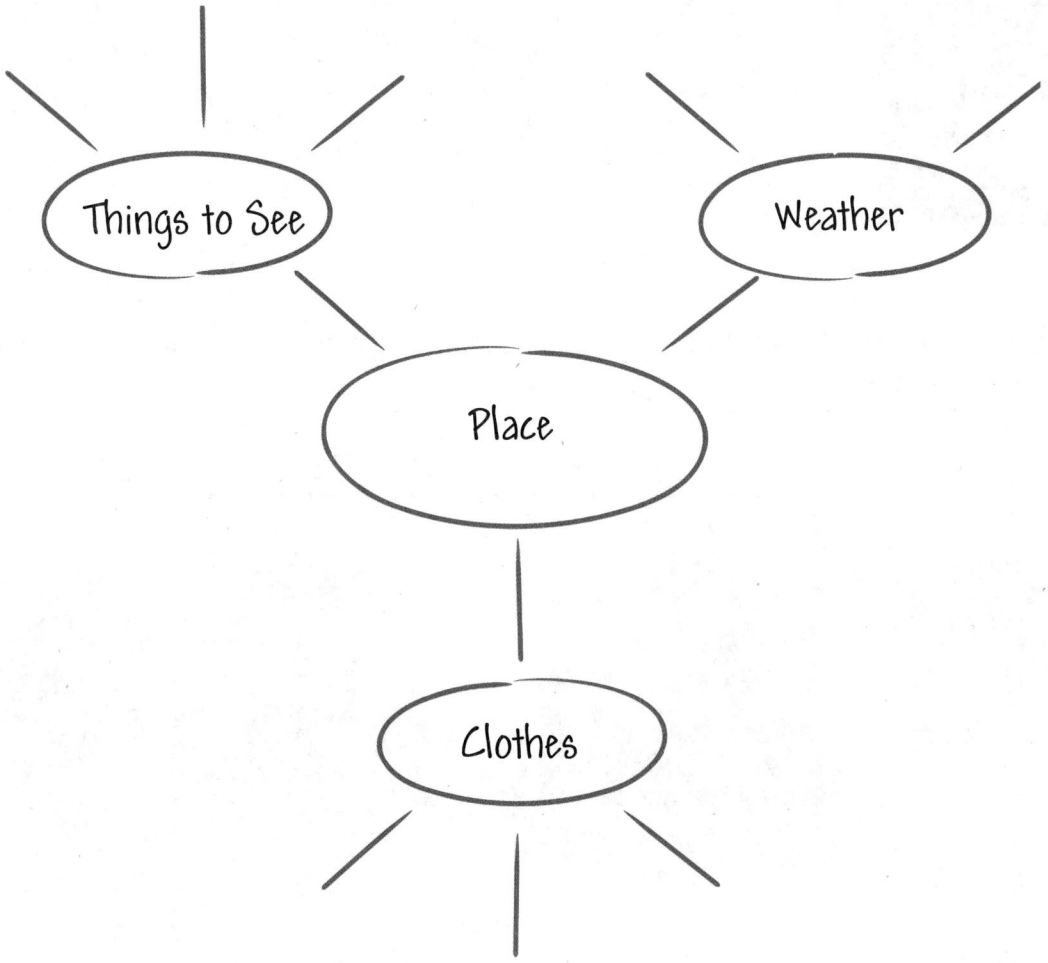

B. Write sentences to describe the place you would like to explore.

_____

_____

_____

_____

_____

© NGSP & HB

Name _____

High Frequency Words, Part 1

A. Read each word. Then write it.

1. places _____
2. important _____
3. world _____
4. always _____
5. or _____

B. Find the new words. Write the words on the lines.

6. These 2 words have a **w**.

always _____ _____

C. Work with a partner. Follow the steps.

- Read aloud each new word in the box.
- Your partner writes the words.
- Have your partner read the words to you.
- Now you write the words on the lines below.
- Read the words to your partner.

7. _____
8. _____
9. _____
10. _____
11. _____

© NGSP & HB

Name _____

High Frequency Words, Part 2

A. Read each word. Then write it.

1. river _____
2. through _____
3. once _____
4. water _____
5. below _____

B. Find the new words in the box. Write the words on the lines.

6. These 2 words have a **w**.

water _____ _____

C. Work with a partner. Follow the steps.

- Read aloud each new word in the box.
- Your partner writes the words.
- Have your partner read the words to you.
- Now you write the words on the lines below.
- Read the words to your partner.

7. _____
8. _____
9. _____
10. _____
11. _____

© NGSP & HB

Name _____

Words with Long *a*

A. Read each word. Which picture goes with the word? Write its letter.

1. tray D
2. stain ___
3. play ___
4. sail ___
5. midday ___
6. train ___

A. 

B. 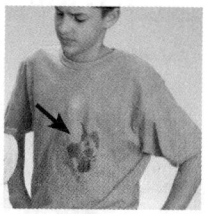

C. 

D. 

E. 

F. 

B. Now read the story. Circle long *a* words with *ai* and *ay*. Write them in the chart. Write each word one time.

My Grandma's Chair

My grandma has a favorite chair. She mainly keeps it upstairs. It has blue and purple flowers in a chain. It is big and soft. When I was little, my grandma let me play in her chair. I would pretend to be an old lady.

My grandma has gray hair, but she likes to do many things. She loves to raise the window shades early in the day. Sometimes, my grandma and I collect daisies. Then she might say, "Now, you may sit in my special chair." I always wait for her to tell me.

7. mainly	12. _____
8. _____	13. _____
9. _____	14. _____
10. _____	15. _____
11. _____	16. _____
	17. _____

© NGSP & HB

Name _____

Words with Long *a*, Long *e*, and Long *o*

A. Read each word. Which picture goes with the word? Write its letter.

1. coast N
2. boat ___
3. train ___
4. braid ___
5. road ___
6. seeds ___
7. paints ___
8. feet ___
9. sail ___
10. tree ___
11. tray ___
12. geese ___
13. crow ___
14. seal ___
15. tea ___

A. 

B. 

C. 

D. 

E. 

F. 

G. 

H. 

I. 

J. 

K. 

L. 

M. 

N. 

O. 

B. Name each picture below. Which words above have the same long vowel sound as the picture name? Write the words on the lines.

16. 

train
_____
_____
_____
_____

17. 

_____
_____
_____
_____
_____
_____

18. 

_____
_____
_____
_____

© NGSP & HB

Name _____

Words with Short and Long Vowels

A. Name each picture. Read the two words. Circle the word that names the picture.

1. 

cot / (coat)

2. 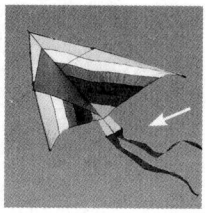

tap / tail

3. 

bed / beach

4. 

sell / seal

5. 

pan / paint

6. 

pens / peas

7. 

cost / coast

8. 

rod / road

B. Now read the story. Circle the words with long *a*. Underline the words with short *a*. Write them in the chart. Write each word one time.

Mom to the Rescue!

Nick (always) goes home to see his mom once a year. He <u>packs</u> his gray bag. What if it rains? Nick gets his coat. What if it's hot? Nick gets his swim trunks. He runs to catch the train, but he forgets his bag! Mom meets Nick in Bay City. She asks, "Where is your bag?" At home, Mom looks through the house. Nick waits. Mom comes back with his old clothes!

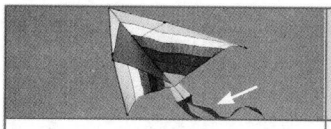	
9. always	15. packs
10. _____	16. _____
11. _____	17. _____
12. _____	18. _____
13. _____	19. _____
14. _____	20. _____

© NGSP & HB

Name _____

Multisyllabic Words

A. Read each word. Write how many syllables it has.

1. 

weekend

2 _____

2. 

crow

_____

3. 

rowboat

_____

4. 

train

_____

5. 

coast

_____

6. 

seashell

_____

7. 

sunset

_____

8. 

stream

_____

B. Now read the story. Circle the words with two syllables. Write each word in the chart one time. Then write the syllables.

At the Seashore

Dean goes to the seashore on weekends. On wet days, Dean wears his raincoat down to the beach. He hunts for seashells and digs for clams. On warm days, he stays on a sailboat with his dad. They sail from sunrise to sunset. Dean loves his weekends at the seashore.

Word	Syllables	
9. seashore	sea	shore
10.		
11.		
12.		
13.		
14.		
15.		

© NGSP & HB

Name _____

Build Reading Fluency

▶ Phrasing

A. When you read, pause between groups of words that go together.

Stay in your seat / while we move through the water. //
This is an important place / for animals, / too. //

B. Listen to the story. When you hear a short pause, write a / . When you hear a long pause, write //.

Example: Welcome to Black Creek Wetland. // What a great way to spend / a Sunday afternoon. //

Explore a Wetland

Welcome to Black Creek Wetland. What a great way to spend a Sunday afternoon! My name is Jean Clay. I am your guide. Step into the rowboat. Stay in your seat while we move through the water.

Canada has many wetlands. Black Creek Wetland is one of them. A wetland is a low, wet place. Rainwater and many streams or rivers keep it wet. Black Creek is on the shore of Lake Ontario. Plants such as reeds and cattails grow here. This is an important place for animals, too. Ducks and geese lay their eggs here in May.

Sometimes, people drain the water from wetlands. Then they use the land to grow wheat or other crops. Not here. We plan to keep this wetland for the ducks, geese, and other animals.

C. Now read the story to a partner. Read groups of words together. Make a short pause when you see a /. Make a long pause when you see a // .

© NGSP & HB

Name _____

Special Places, Special People

▶ Capitalization: Proper Nouns

A. A proper noun names one particular person, place, or thing.

A proper noun begins with a capital letter.

name of a person	**Sabrina** helps kids at a summer camp.
name of a special place, a city, or a country	She works at **Camp Bellwood** in **Cloverdale**, **New York**.
name of a month or a day	Camp begins on **Saturday**, **June** 30.

B. Read each sentence. Circle the letters that should be capital letters.

1. Camp bellwood is in cloverdale, New York.
2. It is near sutter mountain.
3. Many campers come from boston, massachusetts.
4. They learn to swim at lake bronson.
5. Their teacher is mindy lee.
6. Sabrina and jamal take campers on a hike through the forest.
7. There is a big party at camp on thursday, july 4.
8. On Wednesday, july 10, the campers visit Joe taylor at his farm.
9. The next week, Jamal takes them to niagara Falls.
10. Everyone is sorry when camp ends on friday, august 2.

© NGSP & HB

Learn Key Vocabulary

Name _____

The Water Planet: Key Vocabulary

A. Study each word. Circle a number to rate how well you know it. Then complete the chart.

Rating Scale	1	2	3
	I have never seen this word before.	I am not sure of the word's meaning.	I know this word and can teach the word's meaning to someone else.

▲ The **world's surface** is covered by **oceans**.

Key Words	Check Understanding	Deepen Understanding
1 cold (**cōld**) *adjective* **Rating:** 1 2 3	Ice and snow are **cold**. **Yes** **No**	What happens when you are in a cold place? _____ _____ _____ _____
2 ocean (**ō**-shun) *noun* **Rating:** 1 2 3	An **ocean** is smaller than a pond. **Yes** **No**	What would you find in the ocean? _____ _____ _____ _____
3 surface (**sur**-fes) *noun* **Rating:** 1 2 3	Lakes are on Earth's **surface**. **Yes** **No**	Describe Earth's surface in our region. _____ _____ _____ _____

© NGSP & HB

Name _____

The **ocean** near this beach is **warm.** ▶

Key Words	Check Understanding	Deepen Understanding
4 warm (wôrm) *adjective* **Rating:** 1 2 3	Things freeze in **warm** places. **Yes** **No**	Name two warm places _____ _____ _____ _____
5 world (wirld) *noun* **Rating:** 1 2 3	Our **world** has both land and water. **Yes** **No**	What part of the world do you live in? _____ _____ _____ _____

B. Use at least two of the Key Vocabulary words. Tell how you use water every day.

_____

_____

_____

© NGSP & HB

Writing Project

Name _____

Plan and Write

1. What place would you like to write about? _____

2. Look for ideas in books, magazines, or on the Internet. Fill in a concept map.

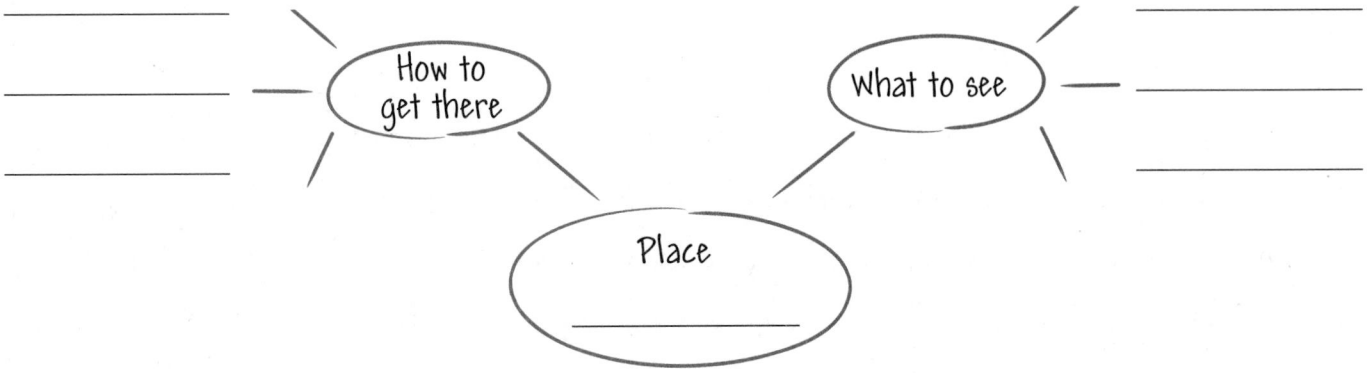

3. Write a title.

4. Write about a place.
   - Use commands.
   - Use adjectives.
   - Tell how to get there.

_____

Take _____ .

Explore _____ .

You can _____ .

_____

_____

_____

_____

_____

5. Copy your sentences onto cards. Attach the cards to a large piece of paper. Add pictures.

© NGSP & HB

Name _____

Check Your Work

Mark Your Changes

∧ **Add.**

≡ **Capitalize.**

▶ Capitalization and Plurals

Read the travel guide. Fix capital letters and plural nouns as needed. Mark your changes. Then write the paragraph correctly.

Visit Florida Now!

Take a trip to sunny Florida! You can learn about space travel at the kennedy Space Center. You can swim at the white sand beaches in fort myers. You can ride on fun rides at disney world. You can see many alligator in the Everglades. Explore florida! There is so much to see and do!

© NGSP & HB

Unit 8 Launch

Name _____

Mind Map

Use the mind map to show ideas about friends and friendship. As you read the selections in this unit, add new ideas you learn about what friends do together.

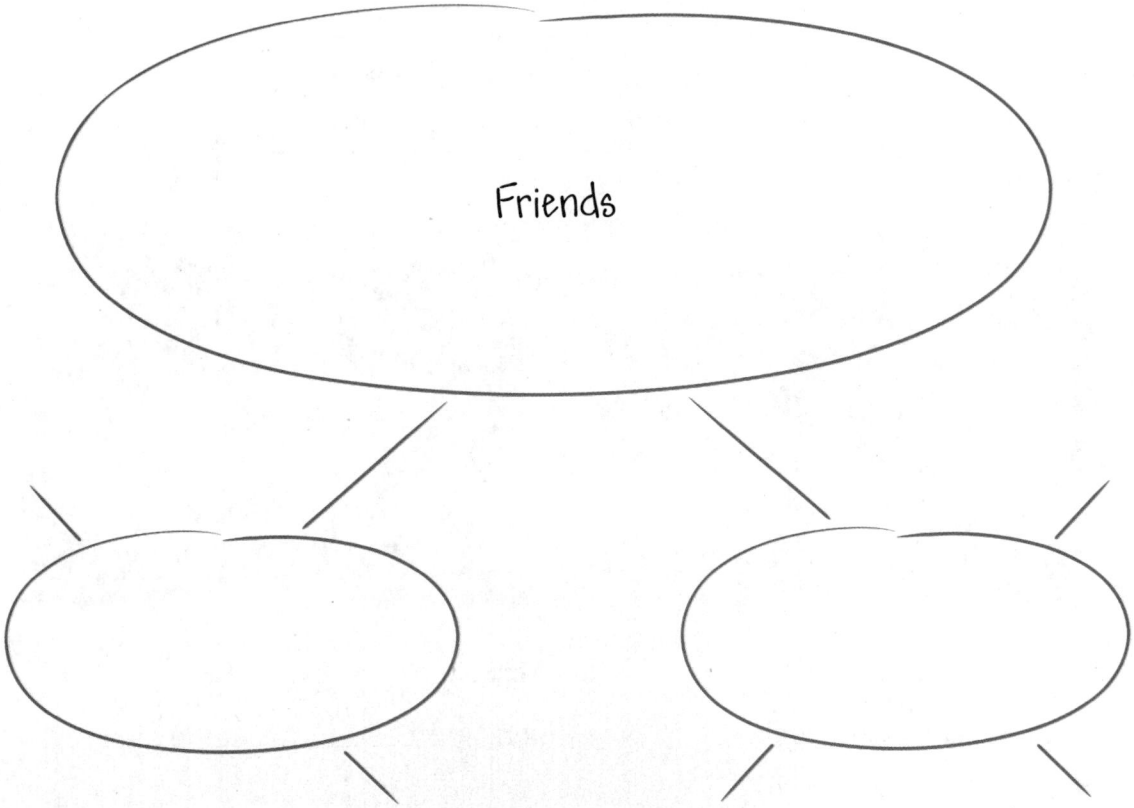

© NGSP & HB

Language Development

Name _____

They Cooked Pizza Together

▶ **Language: Describe Actions**

▶ **Grammar: Past Tense Verbs**

Complete each sentence. Tell what the friends did. Use a verb from the box.

Past Tense Verbs
The **past tense** of a verb tells about an action in the past. Many past tense verbs end in ***-ed***.
Len scratch**ed** his head.

laughed	**helped**	**spilled**	**rolled**
enjoyed	**looked**	**cooked**	**watched**

1.

Miguel ___rolled___ the dough.

Len _____ at the cookbook.

2.

Miguel _____ sauce.

Len _____ about the mess.

3.

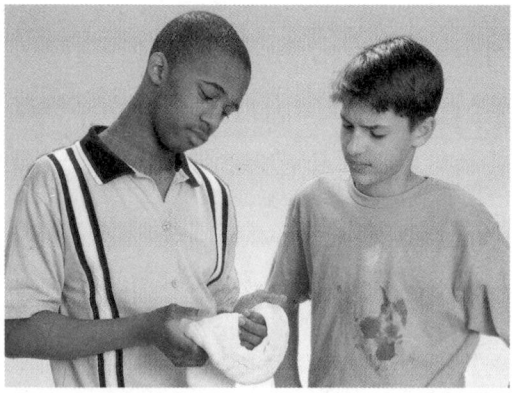

Then Len _____ with the dough.

Miguel _____ him.

4.

Finally, the boys _____ the pizza.

They _____ their dinner.

© NGSP & HB

Language Development

Name _____

How Do They Feel?

▶ **Vocabulary: Feelings**

▶ **Language: Express Feelings**

A. Look at each picture. Tell how the person feels. Use a word from the box.

scared	confused	bored	mad	proud	sad

1. 

confused

2. 

_____

3. 

_____

4. 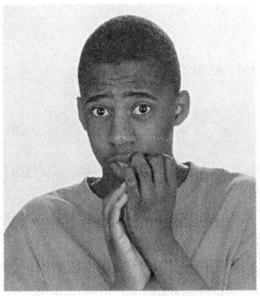

_____

5. 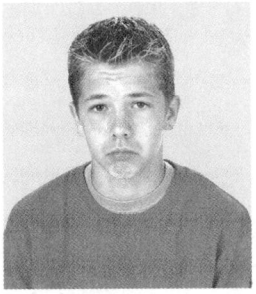

_____

6. 

_____

B. Read each sentence. Tell how you feel.

7. I get a good grade on my test.

   I feel proud .

8. My best friend moves to another city.

   I am _____ .

9. There is nothing for me to do.

   I feel _____ .

10. A bee buzzes around my head.

    I am _____ .

© NGSP & HB

Language Development

Name _____

It Was Fun to Study Together

▶ Grammar: Irregular Past Tense Verbs: *Was* and *Were*

Use *was* and *were* to tell about the past.

Pronoun	Verb	Example
I	was	I **was** in the library.
you	were	You **were** by the bookshelf.
he, she, it	was	It **was** warm in the library.
we	were	We **were** not bored.
they	were	They **were** curious about the magazines.

Use ***There was*** for one person or thing.

Use ***There were*** for two or more.

There was a girl beside me.
There were many books to read.

Complete each sentence. Use *was* or *were*.

1. It ___was___ 1:30.
2. I _____ with my friends.
3. We _____ in the library.
4. Other students _____ there, too.
5. There _____ a new librarian at the desk.
6. Our table _____ not very big.
7. Carol _____ beside me.
8. There _____ good magazines on the shelf.
9. Mr. Smith _____ glad to answer my questions.
10. It _____ fun to study with my friends.

© NGSP & HB

 Name _____

We Weren't There!

▶ Grammar: Negative Sentences and Contractions with *Not*

There are different ways to build negative sentences in the past tense.

Add the word ***not*** after ***was*** and ***were***.

She **was not** happy.

We **were not** on time.

With other verbs, add ***did not*** before the verb.

The movie did not started.

When you add *did not* to a sentence, take the *-ed* off the main verb.

Complete the sentence. Use *did not, was not,* or *were not.*
Then rewrite the sentence. Use a contraction.

Contractions
did + not = didn't
was + not = wasn't
were + not = weren't

1. Kelli was not late.
   Kelli wasn't late.
2. Dina and I _____ there.
   _____
3. We _____ answer the phone.
   _____

4. The bus _____ stop for us.
   _____
5. We _____ on time for the movie.
   _____
6. Kelli _____ happy.
   _____

© NGSP & HB

Name _____

Identify Causes and Effects

▶ Sum It Up

A. Read the passage. Look for causes and effects. Complete the cause-and-effect chart.

The New Kid

Luis felt nervous as he walked into the lunch room. This was his first day at Greenfield Middle School. He didn't know anyone, so he sat at table by himself.

"How will I ever make friends?" he wondered. "All these people already know each other. They've been in school together for two months." Someone settling into the seat beside him interrupted Luis's thoughts.

"Hi, I'm Eduardo," said the boy. "I just started in this school last week, and I don't know anyone." Suddenly, Luis felt much better. He thought Eduardo might be his first new friend at his new school.

Cause-and-Effect Chart

Causes		Effects
It was Luis's first day at a new school.	→	
	→	
	→	
	→	

B. Write a sentence for each cause and effect in the chart. Use the word *because*.

1. _____

2. _____

3. _____

4. _____

© NGSP & HB

Name _____

High Frequency Words, Part 1

A. Read each word. Then write it.

1. saw _____
2. was _____
3. were _____
4. their _____
5. said _____

B. Write the answer to each question. Find the new words in the box. Write the words on the lines.

6. Which 2 words have 3 letters?

   saw _____ _____

7. Which word rhymes with **her**?

   _____

8. Which word has 5 letters?

   _____

9. Which word rhymes with **red**?

   _____

10. Which word is the past tense of **see**?

    _____

© NGSP & HB

Name _____

High Frequency Words, Part 2

A. Read each word. Then write it.

1. began _____
2. about _____
3. dance _____
4. thought _____
5. again _____

B. Write the answer to each question. Find the new words in the box. Write the words on the lines.

6. Which word means "started"?

   began

7. Which word has 7 letters?

   _____

8. Which 3 words have 2 syllables?

   _____ _____ _____

9. Which 4 words have 5 letters each?

   _____ _____

   _____ _____

10. Which word means "once more"?

    _____

© NGSP & HB

Name _____

Verbs with -*ed*

A. Read each sentence. Change the word in dark type to tell about the past.

1. Lin and I ___planted___ seeds.
   (plant)
2. The next day it _____ on our seeds.
   (rain)

3. I _____ her pull the weeds.
   (help)
4. We _____ for the plants to grow.
   (wait)

5. We _____ a lot of peas.
   (pick)
6. We _____ them for our friends.
   (cook)

B. Now read the story. Circle the words with -*ed*. Write each word in the chart one time. Then write the root word.

We Waited for the Sun

On Saturday morning it rained. Kim and I waited for the sun. When it peeked through the clouds, we ran to the beach. We saw some birds and hunted for shells by the water. We cleaned the sand off the shells and put them in a box. Then we hunted for tiny crabs in the sand. Kim lifted one crab so we could see it up close.

Word with -*ed*	Root Word
7. Waited	wait
8.	
9.	
10.	
11.	
12.	

© NGSP & HB

Name _____

Verbs with -*ed*

A. Read each sentence. Change the word in dark type to tell about the past.

1. Lane and I ___planned___ a trip.
   (plan)
2. We _____ some snacks and water.
   (grab)

3. We _____ in the hills for six hours.
   (hike)
4. We laughed and _____ the whole time.
   (joke)

5. We _____ just before dark.
   (stop)
6. Later, we _____ to another friend about the trip.
   (brag)

B. Now read the story. Circle the words with -*ed*. Write each word in the chart one time. Then write the root word.

With a Friend

Ben's feet (dragged) as he jogged in the park. Sometimes he hated to jog by himself. He sat down on a bench to rest. Just then his friend Matt jogged by and waved.

"Matt!" Ben said. "Wait for me!" He hopped up and ran to catch up with Matt. He smiled as they ran side by side. It was more fun to jog with a friend!

Word with -*ed*	Root Word
7. ___dragged___	___drag___
8. _____	_____
9. _____	_____
10. _____	_____
11. _____	_____
12. _____	_____

© NGSP & HB

Name _____

Build Reading Fluency

▶ Phrasing

A. When you read, pause between groups of words that go together.

She looked at the clock / above the stove. //
"Veronica has ten more seconds to get here," / she said. //

B. Listen to the story. When you hear a short pause, write a / .
When you hear a long pause, write //.

Example: Eva was mad. //She tapped her foot. // She looked at the clock / above the stove. //

Eva's Lesson

Eva was mad. She tapped her foot. She looked at the clock above the stove. "Veronica has ten more seconds to get here," she said. Eva waited and waited. Veronica was always late.

They had planned to talk about their dance for the school show. Eva thought Veronica was not very good. She thought Veronica needed a lot of help.

While she waited, Eva played the CD for their dance. She clapped her hands and kicked to the beat. She began to sing. She kicked again. This time, she kicked too high. She slipped and landed on the rug! Just then, Veronica peeked in the kitchen window. She saw Eva and rushed to help her. Eva smiled and rubbed her leg. "I thought you were the one who needed help. Now I know I was the one," she joked.

C. Now read the story to a partner. Read groups of words together. Make a short pause when you see a /. Make a long pause when you see //.

© NGSP & HB

Name _____

Meg's Friends

▶ Possessive Nouns

A. Some nouns show ownership. They end in 's.

Meg**'s** best friend is Helen. Helen**'s** family lives next door. Helen has a brother. Her brother**'s** name is Fred.

B. Complete each sentence. Add 's to the word in dark print.

1. Meg's _____ favorite sport is tennis.
   (Meg)

2. Her _____ favorite game is tennis, too.
   (friend)

3. Meg uses her _____ racket to play tennis.
   (dad)

4. Helen borrows her _____ racket.
   (brother)

5. _____ racket is new.
   (Fred)

6. _____ mom and dad take the girls to the park.
   (Helen)

7. They play tennis in the _____ park.
   (city)

8. Then _____ brother brings the girls home.
   (Helen)

© NGSP & HB

Learn Key Vocabulary

Name _____

Hand in Hand: Key Vocabulary

A. Study each word. Circle a number to rate how well you know it. Then complete the chart.

This player is shouting because he is **angry** about how the game is going. ▶

Rating Scale	1	2	3
	I have never seen this word before.	I am not sure of the word's meaning.	I know this word and can teach the word's meaning to someone else.

Key Words	Check Understanding	Deepen Understanding
❶ **angry** (**āng**-rē) *adjective* **Rating:** 1 2 3	When you feel **angry**, you are mad about something. **Yes** **No**	How do you help yourself feel better after you get angry? _____ _____ _____ _____
❷ **different** (**di**-fur-rent) *adjective* **Rating:** 1 2 3	Friends can have **different** ideas and still like each other. **Yes** **No**	Name two different languages. _____ _____ _____ _____
❸ **friendship** (**frend**-ship) *noun* **Rating:** 1 2 3	**Friendship** develops when people like each other. **Yes** **No**	Name one important thing in a friendship. _____ _____ _____ _____

© NGSP & HB

Name _____

▲ This **group** is made of many **different** people who are all friends.

Key Words	Check Understanding	Deepen Understanding
❹ **group** (groop) *noun* **Rating:** 1 2 3	You can play music in more than one **group**. **Yes** **No**	Describe a group that you belong to. _____ _____ _____ _____
❺ **hoped** (hōpt) *verb* **Rating:** 1 2 3	Many people have **hoped** for world peace. **Yes** **No**	Describe something you have hoped for. _____ _____ _____ _____

B. Use at least two of the Key Vocabulary words. Tell about a time when you learned something from someone from a different group.

_____

_____

_____

© NGSP & HB

Writing Project

Name _____

Plan and Write

1. Think about a time when you did something fun with a friend. What did you do? Where did you do it? How did you feel? Use the chart to answer the questions.

What We Did	Where	My Feelings

2. Write a title.

3. Tell the **names** of your friends in the first sentence.

4. Tell what you did. Use the **past tense**. Tell how you felt. Use **feeling words**.

_____

_____

_____

_____

_____

_____

_____

_____

_____

_____

© NGSP & HB

Name _____

Check Your Work

Mark Your Changes

≡ **Capitalize.**

℘ **Take out.**

▶ Capitalization and Focus

Read the memory story. Fix capital letters as needed. Take out any sentences that are not about the memory. Mark your changes. Then write the story correctly.

A Green Day with Kwami

by Declan O'Carroll

One day Kwami asked me to lunch at his house. Mrs. jones cooked a special meal. I was surprised when i saw the plate. It had green mashed potatoes, green beans, and green eggs! My sister Zeena is a good cook. We ate the green food. It looked funny but tasted good! Then Kwami and i went downtown to the St. patrick's Day parade. Everyone wore green. It was a green day!

_____

_____

_____

_____

_____

_____

_____

_____

_____

_____

_____

_____

_____

_____

© NGSP & HB

Name _____

Mind Map

Use the mind map to show how people celebrate. As you read the selections in this unit, add new ideas you learn about the ways people celebrate around the world.

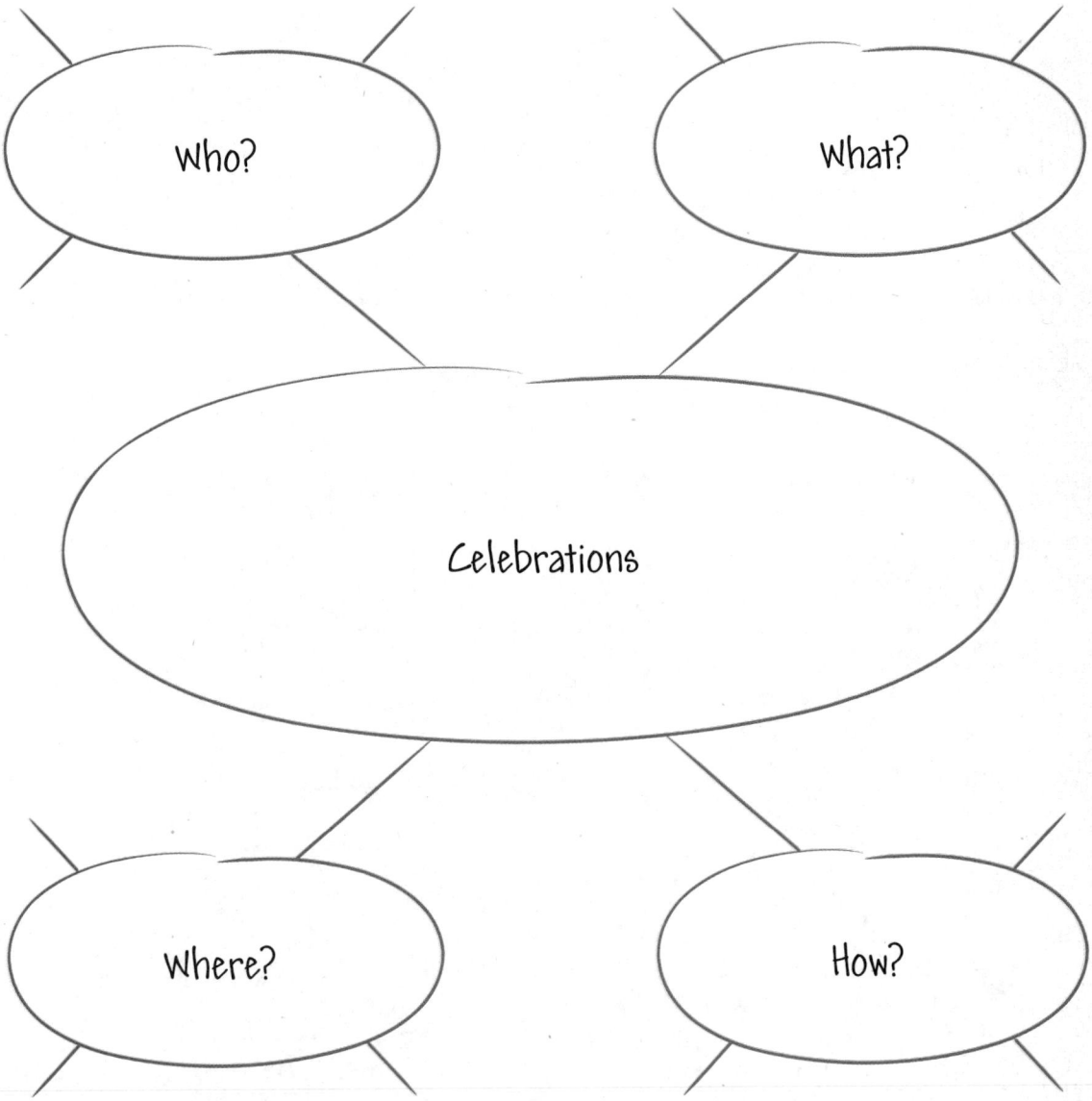

© NGSP & HB

Name _____

How Does He Dance?

▶ **Language: Ask and Answer Questions**

▶ **Grammar: Adverbs**

Look at each picture. Answer the question. Use an adverb from the box.

up	back	high	slowly	forward	now

Adverbs

Many **adverbs** end in -***ly***. They tell how:

turn **quickly**

dance **wildly**

Other adverbs tell when or where:

dance **now**

step **back**

1.

Where does Matt stretch?

Matt stretches ___up___ .

2.

Where does Matt reach?

He reaches _____ .

3.

How does Matt bend?

Matt bends _____ .

4.

Can Matt go back?

No, Matt can't go _____ .

5.

Can Matt jump?

Yes, Matt can jump _____ .

6.

When can he dance?

He can dance _____ .

© NGSP & HB

Name _____

What Are They Doing?

▶ Grammar: Present Progressive Verbs

These verbs tell what is happening now.

The girls **are celebrating** their culture.
They **are standing** in line.
The powwow **is starting** soon.

Complete each sentence. Tell what the people are doing. Use verbs from the box.

are moving	**is stepping**	**are enjoying**	**are playing**
is singing	**are sitting**	**is hopping**	**is listening**

1. The dancer _____ is stepping _____ quickly.
2. His feet _____ forward.
3. He _____ up and down.
4. He _____ to the music.

5. The children _____ in a circle.
6. They _____ the drums.
7. One boy _____ a song.
8. The children _____ the music.

© NGSP & HB

 Name _____

Dancers Around the World

▶ **Vocabulary: Country Words**

▶ **Language: Describe People**

A. Look at each picture. Complete the sentences. Use words from the box.

Scotland	Scottish	Cambodia	Cambodian

1. 

This dancer is from Scotland.

She is _____.

2. 

These dancers are _____.

They are doing a dance from _____.

B. Describe the dancers. Tell what they look like. Tell what they are doing. Complete the sentences.

3. The Scottish dancer is from Scotland.
4. She wears a _____.
5. The dancer is _____.
6. The _____ dancers are sitting.
7. They have _____.
8. These dancers are _____.

© NGSP & HB

Name _____

We Like to Dance!

▶ Grammar: Phrases with *Like To* and *Want To*

Use a verb to complete a phrase with *like to* or *want to*.

like to + verb	want to + verb
They **like to dance** together.	They **want to learn** more steps.
She **likes to step** to the music.	He **wants to teach** people.

Add an -s when you use he, she, or it.

Complete the sentences for each picture. Use *like to* or *want to*.

1.

The students _____ like to _____ leap.

They _____ perform for the Russian ballet.

2.

The boy _____ spin.

He _____ dance fast.

3.

The boys _____ celebrate the Chinese New Year.

They _____ carry the dragon costume.

4.

The dancer from India _____ share a story.

She _____ show it with her dance.

© NGSP & HB

 Name _____

Classify Information

▶ Sum It Up

A. Think about the kind of dancing you like to do. Fill in the concept map. Tell who you dance with, why you dance, where you dance, and how you dance.

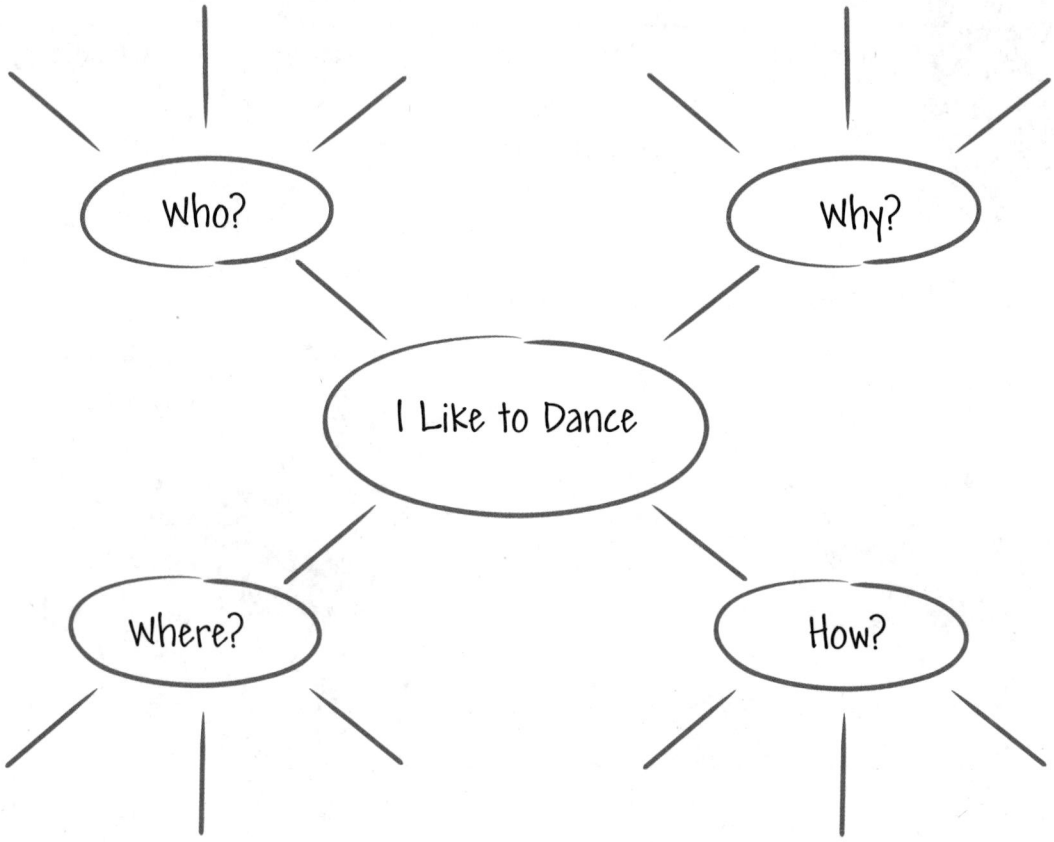

B. Write sentences to tell about the way you like to dance. Use words from your concept map in your sentences.

_____

_____

_____

_____

© NGSP & HB

Name _____

High Frequency Words, Part 1

A. Read each word. Then write it.

1. celebrate _____
2. most _____
3. young _____
4. children _____
5. started _____

B. Write the answer to each question. Find the new words in the box. Write the words on the lines.

6. This word ends in **e**.

   celebrate

7. These 2 words have **st**.

   _____ _____

8. This word is the opposite of **old**.

   _____

9. This word begins with **ch**.

   _____

10. This word is the opposite of **ended**.

    _____

© NGSP & HB

Name _____

High Frequency Words, Part 2

A. Read each word. Then write it.

1. beginning _____
2. change _____
3. another _____
4. only _____
5. following _____

B. Read each sentence. Find the new words in the box. Write the words on the lines.

6. These 2 words end with **ing**.

   following _____ _____

7. This word ends with **e**.

   _____

8. This word has the word **other** in it.

   _____

9. Which word has 4 letters?

   _____

10. This word starts with **f**.

    _____

© NGSP & HB

Name _____

Verbs with *-ing*

A. Read each sentence. Change the word in dark type to tell what is happening right now.

1. They are celebrating summer.
   (celebrate)
2. Some people are _____ trips.
   (take)

3. They are _____ in the pool.
   (swim)
4. They are _____ wet.
   (get)

5. This family is _____ outside.
   (sit)
6. They are _____ a picnic lunch.
   (eat)

B. Now read the story. Circle the words with *-ing*. Write each word in the chart one time. Then write the root word.

Our School Fair

Our school fair is beginning at 2 p.m. We are taking all the games outside. Suddenly, it is raining and we are beginning to get very wet. Most of us are rushing inside. Now we are waiting for the rain to stop. Yes. The sun is shining again. The fair can begin on time.

Word with *-ing*	Root Word
7. beginning	begin
8. _____	_____
9. _____	_____
10. _____	_____
11. _____	_____
12. _____	_____

© NGSP & HB

Name _____

Build Reading Fluency

▶ Phrasing

A. When you read, pause between groups of words that go together.

They are greeting / the Chinese dragon, / which brings good luck. //
People dance / to celebrate an important day / in the family. //

B. Listen to the story. When you hear a short pause, write a / .
When you hear a long pause, write //.

Example: This bride / is having fun at her wedding. //

Dance to Celebrate

People dance to celebrate a holiday. These people are beginning the Chinese New Year with a dance. They are greeting the Chinese dragon, which brings good luck. Nine men inside the costume are lifting the dragon with long poles. Only one man is beating a drum. He is following the dragon.

People dance to celebrate an important day in the family. This bride is having fun at her wedding. Three young men are lifting her in her seat while her husband watches. The family is dancing around them. They are smiling and clapping.

C. Now read the story to a partner. Read groups of words together. Make a short pause when you see a /. Make a long pause when you see a //.

© NGSP & HB

Learn Key Vocabulary

Name _____

Kite Festival: Key Vocabulary

A. Study each word. Circle a number to rate how well you know it. Then complete the chart.

Rating Scale	1	2	3
	I have never seen this word before.	I am not sure of the word's meaning.	I know this word and can teach the word's meaning to someone else.

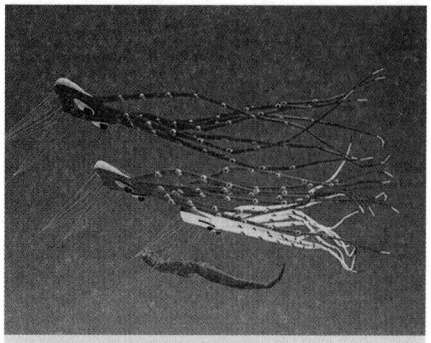

▲ **Colorful** kites fly **gracefully** through the air.

Key Words	Check Understanding	Deepen Understanding
❶ **celebrate** (se-luh-brāt) *verb* **Rating:** 1 2 3	Americans **celebrate** the Fourth of July. **Yes** **No**	How do you celebrate a birthday? _____ _____ _____ _____
❷ **colorful** (cul-er-ful) *adjective* **Rating:** 1 2 3	Gray skies are **colorful**. **Yes** **No**	Which of your clothes are colorful? _____ _____ _____ _____
❸ **enjoy** (en-joi) *verb* **Rating:** 1 2 3	Most people **enjoy** holidays. **Yes** **No**	Tell what you enjoy about one holiday. _____ _____ _____ _____

© NGSP & HB

Name _____

Teams **celebrate** the kite festival by flying a **colorful** kite. ▶

Key Words	Check Understanding	Deepen Understanding
4 gracefully (grās-ful-lē) *adverb* **Rating:** 1 2 3	Ballet dancers move **gracefully**. **Yes** **No**	Describe something that moves gracefully. _____ _____ _____ _____
5 started (stär-ted) *verb* **Rating:** 1 2 3	The day has not **started** yet. **Yes** **No**	Describe how one of your family parties started. _____ _____ _____ _____

B. Use at least two of the Key Vocabulary words. Describe what it would be like to watch the kite festival in Japan.

_____

_____

_____

© NGSP & HB

Writing Project

Name _____

Plan and Write

1. Choose a celebration. _____

2. What do you want to write about? Make a list of questions.

   A. How _____

   B. Where _____

   C. What _____

3. Use your questions to interview someone about the celebration. Write the answers.

   A. _____

   B. _____

   C. _____

4. Write a title.

5. Name the **celebration** and the **country** in the first sentence.

6. Write sentences. Tell what people **like to** do at the celebration.

_____

_____

_____

_____

_____

_____

_____

_____

_____

_____

_____

_____

_____

_____

© NGSP & HB

Name _____

Check Your Work

Mark Your Changes

≡ **Capitalize.**

℘ **Take out.**

▶ Capitalization and Details

Read the blog. Fix capital letters where they are needed. Take out any detail that does not go with the topic. Mark your changes. Then write the blog correctly.

Chinese Lunar New Year

Many people from china celebrate the Lunar New Year. we go to parades where people dress like lions and dragons. There are similar celebrations for the new year in other countries like vietnam. We also go to parades on memorial day and the fourth of July. this celebration is also special because families get together for a reunion dinner and eat special food. Chinese Lunar New Year is celebrated in different months. Sometimes it falls in january. Sometimes it is in february.

© NGSP & HB

Name _____

Timed Reading Chart

How many words did you read correctly for each selection? Complete the chart to show your scores for each day.

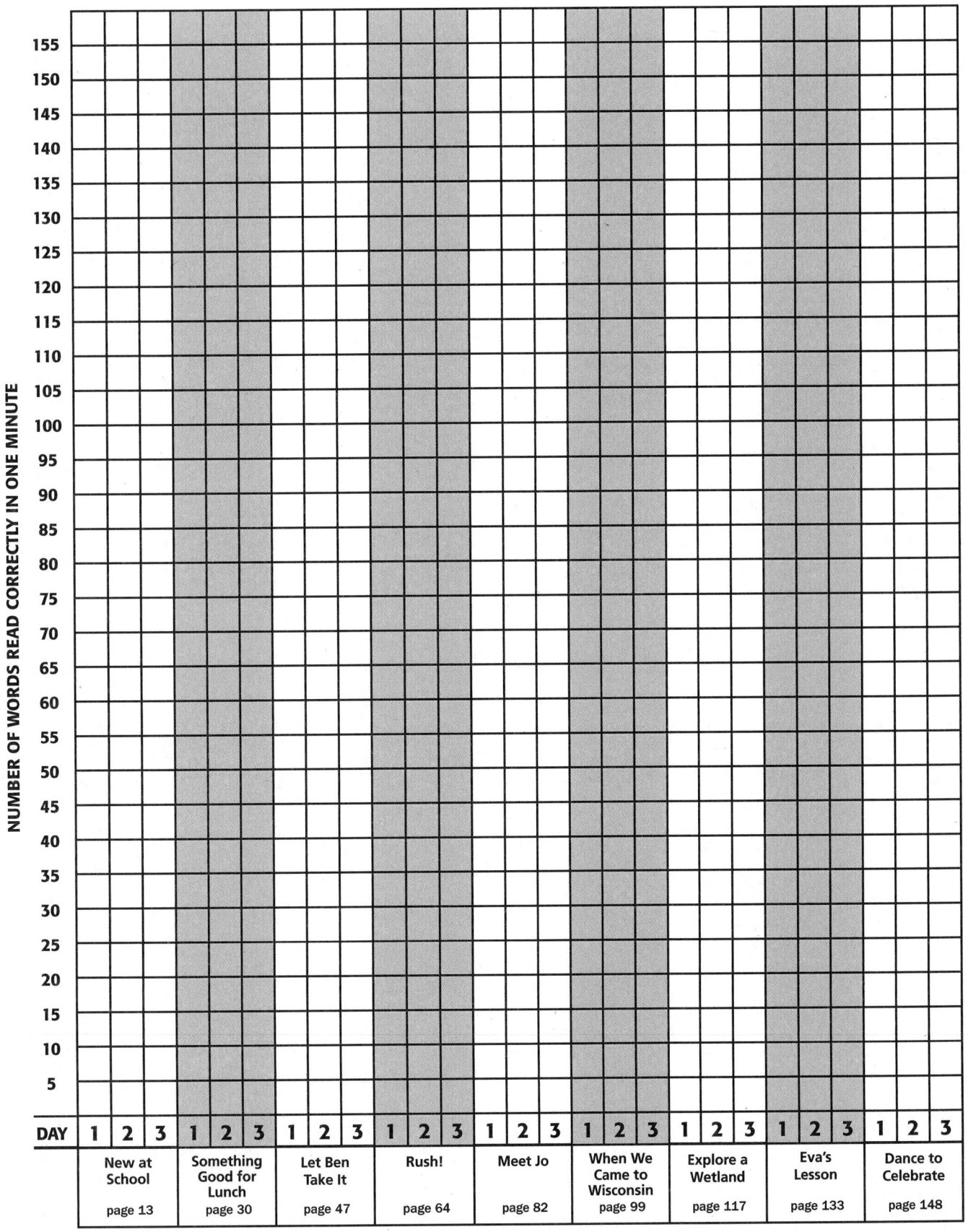

© NGSP & HB

Decodable Stories

Contents

Unit 1

A Bad Day! 155

Unit 2

Pop! 159

Unit 3

Fred at Work 163

Unit 4

From Last to First 167

Unit 5

A City Food Festival 171

Unit 6

At Home 175

Unit 7

On the River 179

Unit 8

About Duke 183

Unit 9

Celebrate the Past 187

This is not a good day!

Words with /ă/a; /ŏ/o			
am	class	lot	tan
and	dad	mad	van
at	ham	mom	
bad	has	not	
bag	hot	sad	
can	jog	stops	

High Frequency Words for Unit 1
home

© NCSP & HB

Short *a* and Short *o*

A Bad Day!

Fold

I am at school at 8:00.
I am at lunch at 12:00.
I have hot ham. I do not like
ham. I am sad and mad.

I jog a lot in P.E.
I am hot! I stop.

I have a class at 8:15. I do not have my tan bag. My tan bag is at home.

Mom is mad. Mom can not come. Dad can.

Dad stops the van. Dad has my tan bag.

© NGSP & HB

It is such a mess! Mom does not like it a bit. Jim just grins.

Words with /ĭ/*i*; /ŭ/*u*; /ch/*ch*, tch			
bag	fills	it	stuff
big	grabs	Jim	such
bit	grins	just	switch
bunch	hits	much	will
but	hunts	pop	
catch	in	rip	
fast	is	snack	

High Frequency Words for Units 1–2		
open	then	there

© NGSP & HB

Short *i*, Short *u*, *ch*, and *tch*

Pop!

Fold

Jim hits the TV switch.

Popcorn fills the room fast!

Jim looks at his snack. Jim can spot a rip in the bag. Jim opens the microwave.

Then Jim hunts for a snack. There is just a bunch of old stuff, but Jim does spot a bag of . . .

It will not take much time.

Jim grabs a bag. He does not spot a rip in the bag.

Jim can mix punch as it pops.

© NGSP & HB

At last, the day ends. Mom has one last job for Fred.

Where is Fred? He is in bed! Zzzzzzzz.

Words with /ĕ/*e*; /sh/*sh*; /k/*ck*			
bed	Fred	mess	stack
chest	fresh	net	trash
docks	gets	picks	when
ends	help	shop	yes

High Frequency Words for Units 1–3		
love	there	want

© NGSP & HB

Short *e*, *sh*, *ck*, and Double Consonants

Fred at Work

Fred loves his job on the docks.
Fred gets to help a lot.

Fred takes trash to a bin.

Fold

Fred picks up the trash.
HISS!
Did you spill this trash? Bad cat!
Here, Fuzz!
This cat will not help.

He helps when there is a mess in the shop.
Do you want me to stack cans?
Yes! Thanks, Fred!

Jill has a batch of fresh fish.
I can help. I will fill the chest with ice.
ICE
FRESH FISH

THE LUNCH SPOT
Fred helps a girl get her hat.
THE LUNCH SPOT
I get a net for jobs like this.

© NGSP & HB

Fold

That day, Fran runs at a track meet. But Fran is not last. Fran is first!

Words with Blends and Digraphs			
bang	from	ring	thinks
catch	kids	rush	track
check	last	sock	which
clock	left	spot	
fast	lunch	still	
Fran	pack	that	

High Frequency Words for Units 1–4		
first	from	want

© NGSP & HB

Blends and Digraphs

From Last to First

Fold

It is 7:00 a.m. on a school day. Fran is still in bed.
Fran! It is 7:00 a.m.!
BANG! BANG!
7:00
Fran will not rush.
Fran jumps on the last step. She is the last kid on the bus.
Fran did it!
Good job!
SCHO

Fold

Fran runs to catch the bus. The kids yell at Fran to run fast. They do not want Fran to miss the bus.
Fran! The bus leaves at 8:00. You need to rush!
Which belt do I want?

Fold

Fran has no time left. Fran still thinks she can catch the bus.

© NGSP & HB

Fold

Word Patterns and Multisyllabic Words			
basket	happens	stand	crab
chips	hundreds	stands	sandwich
chopsticks	is	sum	has
dim	muffins	that	had
Ekram	napkin	this	
festival	Pedro	with	
fish	shish-ke-bob	pumpkin	

High Frequency Words for Units 1–5			
all	first	new	something
city	love	next	there
enough	more	people	want
find	move	second	

© NCSP & HB

Word Patterns and Multisyllabic Words

A City Food Festival

Fold

The city is a great place to be.
Something new happens all the time.
What is this? There are hundreds of people here.
It's the city Food Festival. Come on, Pedro. Let's go!
FISH & CHIPS

Do you want a crab sandwich?
No! Not for me.
CRABS & CLAMS
Pedro has had enough to eat.

The boys are still hungry! They see a man with muffins to sell.

This is Pedro's first time at a food festival.

The boys smell lots of good food. Their second stop is a stand that sells Chinese food.

Next they find a stand that sells Greek food.

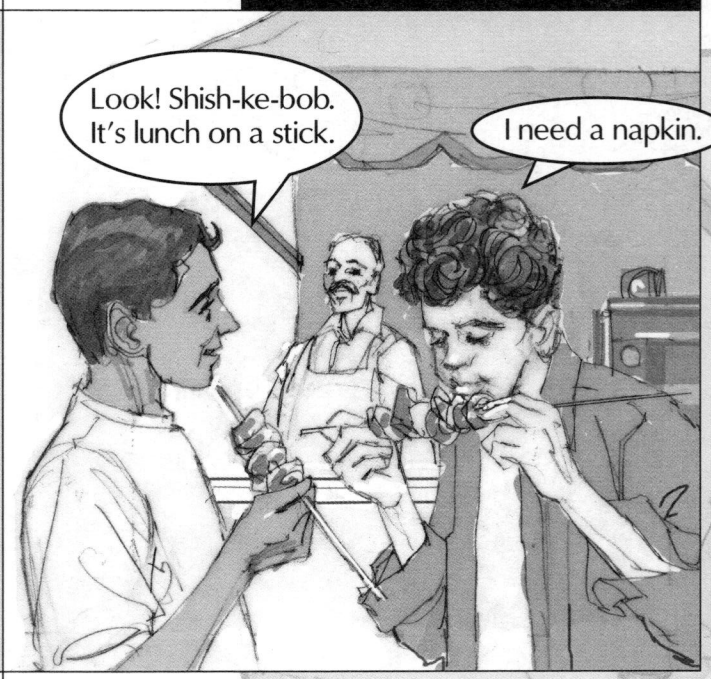

© NGSP & HB

Grandmother likes all the things we do for her. She even likes my brother's drums.

Words with Long Vowels: *a, i, o, u*			
cakes	hope	robe	tune
bake	like	smiles	use
fine	make	take	
home	notes	time	

High Frequency Words for Units 1–6			
all	from	out	wants
down	her	together	
eat	our	something	

© NGSP & HB

Long Vowels: *a, i, o, u*

At Home

My grandmother is here from Japan. Our family is glad to see her. We hope she likes our home.

Soon it is time to eat. We use our best dishes for the food. We take out the best glasses. Then we sit down and eat together. Grandmother smiles and smiles.

Fold

My mother makes crab rolls for Grandmother.

We really like these. I hope she will, too.

We want to make Grandmother glad that she came to see us. So we think of special things to do for her. In Japan, Grandmother does not bake cakes. So I make her one.

It smells good!

My brother wants to do something, too. So he writes some notes for a new tune.
Will Grandmother like this song?
My father puts on his fine silk robe.
Mother will like this.

© NGSP & HB

Fold

It's the end of the day.

Words with Long Vowels: *ai, ay; ee, ea; oa, ow*			
cattail	deep	neat	toad
croak	eats	rain	weekend
day	hears	show	year
daytime	near	sleep	

High Frequency Words for Units 1–7			
always	place	something	there
animals	river	small	water
one			

© NGSP & HB

Long Vowels: *ai, ay; ee, ea; oa, ow* and Compound Words

On the River

Fold

In late June, Shane always spends a weekend with his granddad. This year Granddad takes him to Greenstone River. It's a good place to fish. You can also see a lot of wildlife there.

It's almost sunset. Still no fish. Shane asks if fish like this spot.

Granddad knows the best places to find fish.

They wait for the fish to bite. While they wait, Shane sees something.

Shane hears something in the cattail plants.

© NGSP & HB

Words with Verb Ending *-ed*			
hated	jogged	sailed	waited
hunted	played	stepped	

High Frequency Words for Units 1–8			
about	animals	really	together
again	love	there	was
always	new	thought	were

© NGSP & HB

Verb Ending *-ed*

About Duke

Hi, Chen. You look so sad.
What's wrong? Are you okay?
I really miss Duke. He was my best friend in L.A.

Duke hated to go to the vet for check-ups, but he always sat still for his shots.
Duke went to a vet? I thought vets only checked animals.
Maybe you can call Duke to see how he is, Chen.
BREEDS

LIBRARY
Duke even liked to sit with me and look at books.
We love books. Let's find some books to read together.
LIBRARY

Before I came here, Duke and I were always together. He waited for me after school. He was there to greet me when I stepped off the bus.

Duke and I went to the beach a lot. We sailed together and jogged in the sand. We played ball and hunted for shells.
Well, we can't sail here, but we can jog with you in the park.
We can play ball at the park, too.

© NGSP & HB

Words with Verb Ending *-ing*			
beginning	joking	singing	thinking
dressing	pinning	slapping	throwing
eating	playing	taking	
getting	scrubbing	tasting	

High Frequency Words for Units 1–9			
another	come	really	want
celebrate	people	something	young
city			

© NCSP & HB

Verb Ending *-ing*

Celebrate the Past

My friends are taking me to a fair. It is like a trip back in time.

A play is beginning, and the actors are speaking to me! They ask me to come on the stage and be the queen!

We are eating very odd food today. Todd is tasting something called "toad in the hole." I am feasting on "beef on a stick."

People are dressing in costumes. We want to dress up, too. Sam has a velvet cap. Todd is pinning a ribbon on another hat.

They are playing tunes just like people played 400 years ago! A young man is twirling sticks.

Some women are scrubbing clothes in a stream. They are joking and slapping the cloth on rocks.

© NGSP & HB

Photographs

F2 Row 1: (l, lml) Getty Images, (ml) Digital Stock, (rmr, mr) Getty Images, (r) Artville. Row 2: (l) Ryan McVay/Getty Images, (m) Digital Stock, (r) Metaphotos. Row 3: (l) LWA/Getty Images, (m) Harald Sund/Getty Images, (r) Getty Images. Row 4: (l) Steve Cole/Getty Images, (m) Paul Beard/Getty Images, (r) Getty Images. **F3** Row 1: (l, m) Getty Images, (r) Paul Beard/Getty Images. Row 2: (l) Getty Images, (m) EyeWire, (r) Digital Stock. Row 3: (l) Getty Images, (m) Metaphotos, (r) Getty Images. Row 4: (l, m) Digital Stock, (r) Getty Images. Row 5: (l) Artville, (m) Steve Cole/Getty Images, (r) Getty Images. **F4** (tl, tr) Liz Garza Williams, (bl) Digital Stock, (br) Liz Garza Williams. **F5** Row 1: (l, r) Artville: Row 2: (l) Artville, (r) Liz Garza Williams. Row 3: (l, r) Artville. **F6** (t, m) Liz Garza Williams, (b) Artville. **F7** (t, m) Artville, (b) Liz Garza Williams. **F8** Row 1: (l) Artville. Row 2: (l) Getty Images, (r) Liz Garza Williams. Row 3: (l) Artville, (r) Liz Garza Williams. Row 4: (l) Liz Garza Williams, (r) Artville. Row 5: (l, r) Liz Garza Williams. **F9** Row 1: (l) Getty Images, (r) Liz Garza Williams. Row 2: (l) Liz Garza Williams. Row 3: (l) Artville, (r) Liz Garza Williams. Row 4: (l, r) Liz Garza Williams. **F10** Row 1: (l) Image Club, (ml) Janis Christie/Getty Images, (m) Artville, (mr) Liz Garza Williams, (r) John Paul Endress. Row 2: (l) Getty Images, (m) John Paul Endress, (r) Stockbyte. Row 3: (l) John Paul Endress, (m) Artville, (r) Stockbyte. Row 4: (l) Digital Stock, (m) Getty Images, (r) Liz Garza Williams. Row 5: (l) Artville, (m) John Paul Endress, (r) Liz Garza Williams. **F11** Row 1: (l) Artville, (m) D. Falconer/PhotoLink/Getty Images, (r) Getty Images. Row 2: (l) Getty Images, (m) Stockbyte/Getty Images, (r) Liz Garza Williams. Row 3: (l) John Paul Endress, (m) Stockbyte, (r) Liz Garza Williams. Row 4: (l) Liz Garza Williams, (m) Stockbyte, (r) Getty Images. **F15** (t-b) Stockbyte, John Paul Endress, New Century Graphics, Stockbyte/Getty Images. **F16** Row 1: (l) Liz Garza Williams, (r) D. Falconer/PhotoLink/Getty Images. Row 2: (l, r) Liz Garza Williams. Row 3: (l) Stockbyte, (r) John Paul Endress. Row 4: (l, ml) Getty Images, (mr) John Paul Endress, (r) D. Falconer/PhotoLink/Getty Images. Row 5: (l) Artville, (ml, mr, r) Liz Garza Williams, (br) Artville. **F17** Row 1: (l) Artville, (r) Stockbyte. Row 2: (l) Getty Images, (r) John Paul Endress. Row 3: (l) Liz Garza Williams, (r) D. Falconer/PhotoLink/Getty Images. Row 4: (l) Paul Beard/Getty Images, (ml) D. Falconer/PhotoLink/Getty Images, (mr, r) Liz Garza Williams. Row 5: (l) Digital Stock, (ml) Stockbyte, (mr) Getty Images, (r) Liz Garza Williams. Row 6: (l, ml) Liz Garza Williams, (mr) Stockbyte/Getty Images, (r) Liz Garza Williams. **F18** Row 1: (l) Getty Images, (ml) Liz Garza Williams, (m) Getty Images, (mr) Artville, (r) Liz Garza Williams. Row 2: (l) SuperStock, Inc/SuperStock, (ml) John Paul Endress, (mr) Ryan McVay/Getty Images, (r) Image Club. Row 3: (l, ml) Artville, (mr) C Squared Studios/Getty Images, (r) John Paul Endress. Row 4: (l) John Paul Endress, (ml) Stockbyte, (mr) John Paul Endress, (r) Jack Fields/Corbis. Row 5: (l) Artville, (ml) Stockbyte, (mr) EyeWire, (r) Artville. **F19** Row 1: (l) John Paul Endress, (m) Artville, (r) Liz Garza Williams. Row 2: (l) Getty Images, (m) Digital Stock, (r) Stockbyte. Row 3: (l) Laura Dwight/Corbis, (m) Liz Garza Williams, (r) D. Falconer/PhotoLink/Getty Images. Row 4: (l, m) Getty Images, (r) John Paul Endress. **F20** Liz Garza Williams. **F23** (t-b) Artville, Getty Images, Bill Aron/PhotoEdit, D. Falconer/PhotoLink/Getty Images, Liz Garza Williams. **F24** Row 1: (l) Liz Garza Williams, (m) Stockbyte, (r) Laura Dwight/Corbis. Row 2: (l) Getty Images, (m, r) John Paul Endress. Row 3: (l) Getty Images, (m) D. Falconer/PhotoLink/Getty Images, (r) Getty Images. Row 4: (l) Artville, (m) Thom Lang/Corbis. Row 5: (l, m) Getty Images, (r) Liz Garza Williams. **F25** Row 1: (l) Bill Aron/PhotoEdit, (m) John Paul Endress, (r) Liz Garza Williams. Row 2: (m) Stockbyte, (r) C Squared Studios/Getty Images. Row 3: (l) Laura Dwight/Corbis, (m, r) Artville. Row 4: (l) Laura Dwight/Corbis, (ml) Getty Images, (mr, r) Liz Garza Williams. Row 5: (l) D. Falconer/PhotoLink/Getty Images, (ml) Ryan McVay/Getty Images. Row 6: (l, ml) Getty Images, (mr) C Squared Studios/Getty Images, (r) Stockbyte/Getty Images. **F26** (l, m) Liz Garza Williams. (mr) Getty Images, (r) Digital Studios. **F27** Row 1: (l) Laura Dwight/Corbis, (m) John Paul Endress, (r) Liz Garza Williams. Row 2: (l) Liz Garza Williams, (m) John Paul Endress, (r) Getty Images. Row 3: (l) C Squared Studios/Getty Images, (m) Artville, (r) Charles Krebs/Getty Images. Row 4: (l) Digital Studios, (m) Duomo/Corbis, (r) Liz Garza Williams. **F31** (t) Duomo/Corbis, (m) C Squared Studios/Getty Images, (b) David Young-Wolff/PhotoEdit. **F32** Row 1: (l) C Squared Studios/Getty Images. (ml, mr) Liz Garza Williams, (r) David Young-Wolff/PhotoEdit. Row 2: (l, m) Artville, (r) C Squared Studios/Getty Images. Row 3: (l) John Paul Endress, (m, r) Getty Images. Row 4: (l, ml) Liz Garza Williams, (mr) Artville, (r) David Young-Wolff/PhotoEdit. Row 5: (m, r) Liz Garza Williams. Row 6: (l) D. Falconer/PhotoLink/Getty Images, (m) Ryan McVay/Getty Images, (r) Laura Dwight/Corbis. **F33** Row 1: (l, ml) Liz Garza Williams, (mr) Getty Images, (r) John Paul Endress. Row 2: (l) Getty Images, (m) Bill Aron/PhotoEdit, (r) D. Falconer/PhotoLink/Getty Images. Row 3: (l) Getty Images, (m) Laura Dwight/Corbis, (r) Liz Garza Williams. Row 4: (l) Getty Images, (m) C Squared Studios/Getty Images, (r) Duomo/Corbis. Row 5: (l) Charles Krebs/Getty Images, (m) John Paul Endress, (r) Liz Garza Williams. Row 6: (l) David Young-Wolff/PhotoEdit, (m) Digital Stock, (r) Artville. **F34** (l-ml) John Paul Endress, (m) Image Library, (mr) Artville, (r) John Paul Endress. **F35** Row 1: (l) Liz Garza Williams, (m) Getty Images. Row 2: (l) Roger Ressmeyer/Corbis, (m) New Century Graphics, (r) John Paul Endress. Row 3: (l) Siede Preis/Getty Images, (m) Liz Garza Williams. Row 4: (l) John Paul Endress, (m) Liz Garza Williams, (r) Jack Fields/Corbis. **F39** (t-b) Roger Ressmeyer/Corbis, Liz Garza Williams, Jack Fields/Corbis, Getty Images, Liz Garza Williams, Paul Beard/Getty Images. **F40** Row 1: (l, m) Getty Images, (r) John Paul Endress, Row 2: (l) Ryan McVay/Getty Images, (m) Liz Garza Williams, (r) Siede Preis/Getty Images. Row 3: (l) Bill Aron/PhotoEdit, (r) Jack Fields/Corbis. Row 4: (l) Liz Garza Williams, (m) Roger Ressmeyer/Corbis, (r) John Paul Endress. Row 5: (l) Liz Garza Williams, (m) Getty Images, (r) D. Falconer/PhotoLink/Getty Images. **F41** Row 1: (m) Bill Aron/PhotoEdit, (r) Stockbyte. Row 2: (l-r) Getty Images. Row 3: (l) Getty Images, (m) C Squared Studios/Getty Images, (r) Getty Images. Row 4: (l) New Century Studios, (ml) Getty Images, (mr) Roger Ressmeyer/Corbis, (r) Artville. Row 5: (l, m) Liz Garza Williams, (r) Siede Preis/Getty Images. Row 6: (l) Liz Garza Williams, (ml) Paul Beard/Getty Images, (mr) John Paul Endress, (r) Stockbyte. **5** (tl) Image Club, (tr) Liz Garza Williams, (bl) Getty Images, (br) Image Library. **9** Row 1: (l) Liz Garza Williams, (ml) Bill Aron/PhotoEdit, (mr) Laura Dwight/Corbis, (r) Getty Images. Row 2: (l) Liz Garza Williams, (ml, mr) Getty Images, (r) Stockbyte. Row 3: (m) Getty Images, (r) Liz Garza Williams. **10** Row 1: (l) Getty Images, (ml) Burke/Triolo Products/Brand X/Corbis, (mr, r) Getty Images. Row 2 (l) Bill Aron/PhotoEdit, (ml, mr, r) Getty Images. Row 3: (m, r) Getty Images. **11** Row 1: (l) Digital Stock, (ml) Getty Images, (m) John Paul Endress, (mr) Digital Stock. (r) Joel Satore/National Geographic Image Collection. Row 2: (l) William Salaza/Corbis, (ml) Artville, (m, mr) Getty Images, (r) Michael Jan/Getty Images. Row 3: (l) C Squared Studios/Getty Images, (ml) Getty Images, (m) Jack Fields/Corbis, (mr) Digital Stock, (r) Ryan McVay/Getty Images. Row 4: (l) Liz Garza Williams, (m) Artville, (r) Getty Image. **12** Row 1: (l) Artville, (ml) Getty Images, (m) Michael Yamashita/Corbis, (mr, r) Liz Garza Williams. Row 2: (l) Michael Jang/Getty Images. (ml) Bill Aron/PhotoEdit, (m) Getty Images, (mr) Bob Rowan/Corbis, (r) Getty Images. Row 3: (l) Digital Stock, (ml) James Balog/Getty Images, (m) Getty Images, (mr) Artville, (r) Duomo/Corbis. Row 4: (l, ml) Getty Images, (mr) C Squared Studios/Getty Images, (r) Getty Images. Row 5: (l) C Squared Studios/Getty Images, (ml) Burke/Triolo Productions/Brand X/Corbis, (mr) Michael Yamashita/Corbis, (r) Liz Garza Williams. **13** (tl) Liz Garza Williams. **15** (tr) Hola Images/Getty Images. **16** (tr) David Young-Wolff/Getty Images. **20** Row 1: (l) Getty Images, (m) Felisha Martinez/PhotoEdit, (r) Artville. Row 2: (l) Getty Images, (m) Stockbyte. **26** Row 1: (l) D. Falconer/PhotoLink/Getty Images, (ml, mr) Getty Images, (r) Liz Garza Williams. Row 2: (l) Digital Stock, (mr) Getty Images, (r) Liz Garza Williams. Row 3: (m, r) Liz Garza Williams. **27** (l) John Paul Endress, (ml) Liz Garza Williams, (mr) D. Falconer/PhotoLink/Getty Images, (r) Liz Garza Williams. Row 2: (l, ml) Getty Images, (mr) New Century Graphics, (r) Getty Images. Row 3: (m) Getty Images, (r) New Century Graphics. **28** Row 1: (l) John Paul Endress, (ml, m) Getty Images, (mr) Digital Stock, (r) John Paul Endress. Row 2: (l) John Paul Endress, (ml, m) Getty Images, (mr) John Paul Endress, (r) Getty Images. Row 3: (l) D. Falconer/PhotoLink/Getty Images, (ml) James Marshall/Corbis, (m) Getty Images, (mr) Javier Pierini/Getty Images, (r) New Century Graphics. Row 4: (l, ml) Liz Garza Williams, (mr) Alfred Gescheidt/Getty Images, (r) Artville. Row 6: (l) Getty Images, (m) Artville, (r) Getty Images. **29** Row 1: (l) John Paul Endress, (r) Liz Garza Williams. Row 2: (l) Liz Garza Williams. Row 3: (l, r) Liz Garza Williams. Row 4: (l) Getty Images, (ml) Liz Garza Williams, (mr) Getty Images, (r) D. Falconer/PhotoLink/Getty Images. Row 5: (l) Stockbyte/Getty Images, (ml) Liz Garza Williams, (mr) John Paul Endress, (r) Liz Garza Williams. Row 6: (l) Getty Images, (ml) John Paul Endress, (mr) Digital Stock, (r) Paul Beard/Getty Images. **30** (tl) Liz Garza Williams. **32** (tr) Getty Images, (m) iStockphoto, (b) Burazin/Getty Images. **33** (tr) StockFood/Getty Images. **37** Row 1: (l) Andrea Pistolesi/Getty Images, (m) Paul Conklin/PhotoEdit, (r) Liz Garza Williams. Row 2: (l) Ken Fisher/Getty Images, (m) David Young-Wolff/Getty Images, (r) Walter Hodges/Getty Images. **43** Row 1:(l) Digital Studios, (m) John Paul Endress, (r) Steve Cole/Getty Images, Row 2:

© NGSP & HB

(l) Liz Garza Williams, (m) Getty Images, (r) Stockbyte/Getty Images,. Row 3: (l) Charles Krebs/Getty Images, (m) Getty Images, (r) Liz Garza Williams. **44** Row 1: (l) Myrleen Ferguson Cate/PhotoEdit, (ml) David Young-Wolff/ PhotoEdit, (mr, r) Artville. Row 2: (l) John Paul Endress, (ml) Louis Grandadam/Getty Images, (mr) LWA-Dann Tardif/Corbis, (r) David Hanover/ Getty Images. Row 3: (l, ml) Liz Garza Williams, (mr) John Paul Endress, (r) Michael Newman/ PhotoEdit. Row 4: (l) David Frazier/Corbis, (m) Getty Images. **45** Row 1: (l) Getty Images, (ml, mr, r) John Paul Endress. Row 2: (l) Joel Sartore/ National Geographic Image Collection, (ml) Eising Food Photography/StockFood, (mr) Peter Correz/Getty Images, (r) EyeWire. Row 3: (l) Robert Bremnel/PhotoEdit, (ml) Bob Elsdale/ Getty Images, (mr) Joel Sartore/National Geographic Image Collection, (r) EyeWire. Row 4: (l) Artville, (m) John Paul Endress. **46** Row 1: (l) Liz Garza Williams, (m) Getty Images, (r) Siede Preis/Getty Images. Row 2: (l) Steve Mason/Getty Images, (m) Getty Images, (r) Digital Stock. **47** (tl) Rudi Von Briel/PhotoEdit. **49** (tr) Ken Lucas/ Visuals Unlimited. **50** (tr) Richard T. Nowitz/ Corbis. **52** (tr) LWA-Dann Tardif/Corbis. **61** Row 1: (l) Getty Images, (ml) C Squared Studios/Getty Images, (mr) Getty Images, (r) Artville. Row 2: (l) Steve Mason/Getty Images, (ml) Getty Images, (mr) Michael Jang/Getty Images, (r) Jules Frazier/ Getty Images. **62** Row 1: (l) John Paul Endress, (m) Stockbyte, (r) Getty Images. Row 2: (l) Getty Images, (m) Digital Stock, (r) Paul Beard/Getty Images. **63** Row 1: (l) Digital Stock, (ml) Leonard de Selva/Corbis, (mr) Artville, (r) Getty Images. Row 2: (l) Getty Images, (ml) Digital Stock, (mr) Siede Preis/Getty Images, (r) Phillippa Lewis/ Edivice/Corbis. **66** (tr) Gabriela Median/ SuperStock. **67** (tr) Dany Leham/Corbis. **69** (tr) Cartesia. **72** (tl) Courtesy of Brown Publishing Network, (tr) Daivd Young Wolff/Getty Images, (ml, mr) Courtesy of Brown Publishing Network. **73** Row 1: (l, r) Ronnie Kaufman/Corbis. Row 2: (l, m) Liz Garza Williams, (r) Michael Newman/ PhotoEdit. Row 3: (l, m, r) Liz Garza Williams. **78** Row 1: (l) Jon Smyth/SuperStock, (m) Artville, (r) Barbara Penoyar/Getty Images. Row 2: (l) Carl & Ann Purcell/Corbis, (m) John Paul Endress, (r) Digital Stock. Row 3: (m) Carl & Ann Purcell/ Corbis, (r) John Paul Endress. **79** (l) Getty Images, (ml, mr) Liz Garza Williams, (r) Stockbyte/Getty Images. **80** (tl) Getty Images, (tc) John Paul Endress, (tr) John Foster/Photo Researchers, Inc., (ml) John Paul Endress, (mc) Stockbyte, (mr) Image Club, (bc) John Paul Endress, (br) Stockbyte. **81** Row 1: (l, ml) Artville, (mr) Digital Studios, (r) Getty Images. Row 2: (l) Leonard de Selva/Corbis, (ml) Artville, (mr) New Century Graphics, (r) Michael Newman/ PhotoEdit. **82** (tl) Liz Garza Williams. **83** (tl) Getty Images, (br) Jeff Greenberg/PhotoEdit. **84** (tr) Charlie Dass/SuperStock. **85** (tr) Sal Maimone/SuperStock. **90** (tl) David Young-Wolff/ PhotoEdit, (ml) Michale Newman/PhotoEdit, (mr) Tony Freeman/PhotoEdit, (bl) Michael Newman/PhotoEdit, (br) John Lawlor/Getty Images. **91** (tl, tr, ml, mr) Liz Garza Williams. **95** Row 1: (l) Metaphotos, (ml) Robert Daly/Getty Images, (mr) C Squared Studios/Getty Images, (r) Artville. Row 2: (l) Spike Mafford/Getty Images, (ml) John Paul Endress, (mr) Getty Images, (r) Image Library. Row 3: (m) Artville, (r) Spike Mafford/Getty Images. **96** Row 1: (l) Stephen Simpson/Getty Images, (ml) Artville, (mr, r) Getty Images. Row 2: (l) Getty Images, (ml) Artville, (mr) Roderick Chen/Super/Stock, (r) John Paul Endress. Row 3: (m) Stephen Simpson/Getty Images, (r) Getty Images. Row 4: (m) Artville, (r) Getty Images. **97** Row 1: (l) Ryan McVay/getty Images, (ml) John Paul Endress, (mr) Roderick Chen/SuperStock, (r) Michale Dunn/Corbis. Row 2: (l) Getty Images, (ml) Liz Garza Williams, (mr) Nancy R. Cohen/Getty Images, (r) Metaphotos. Row 3: (m) Getty Images, (r) Nancy R. Cohen/ Getty Images. Row 4: (m) Roderick Chen/ SuperStock, (r) John Paul Endress. **98** Row 1: (l) Liz Garza Williams, (ml, mr) Getty Images, (r) James Forte/Getty Images. Row 2: (l) Getty Images, (ml) Artville, (mr) Liz Garza Williams, (r) Getty Images. **99** (tl) Liz Garza Williams. **101** (tr) Digital Vision/Alamy. **102** (tr) Tony Freeman/ PhotoEdit. **108** (ml, bl) Liz Garza Williams. **109** (tl) Getty Images. Row 1: (l) Digital Stock, (ml) Liz Garza Williams, (mr) Richard Hutchings/ PhotoEdit, (r) Brian Bailey/Getty Images. **113** Row 1: (l, m) Getty Images, (r) Liz Garza Williams, Row 2: (l) Liz Garza Williams, (m) Artville, (r) Bruce Hands/Getty Images. Row 3: (m) Getty Images, (r) Liz Garza Williams. **114** Row 1: (l) Getty Images, (ml) Artville, (m) ©Zdorov Kirill Vladimirovich/Shutterstock, (mr) Jerry Tobias/Corbis, (r) Liz Garza Williams. Row 2: (l) Bruce Hands/Getty Images, (ml, m) Getty Images, (mr) PurestockSuperStock, (r) Felicia Martinez/PhotoEdit. Row 3: (l) ©Creatas/ Jupiterimages, (ml) Joe Munroe/Photo Researchers, (m) Don Mason/Brand X/Jupiter Images, (mr) Digital Stock, (r) Corel. Row 4: (m) SuperStock, (r) Ariel Skelley/Corbis. **115** Row 1: (l) Getty Images, (ml) Roderick Chen/SuperStock, (mr) David Young-Wolff/PhotoEdit, (r) Corel. Row 2: (l) Getty Images, (ml) Okapia Frankfurt/Photo Researchers Inc., (mr) Digital Stock, (r) Nancy R. Cohen/Getty Images. Row 3: (m) Roderick Chen/ SuperStock, (r) Getty Images. **116** Row 1: (l) John Paul Endress, (ml) Don Mason/Brand X/ Jupiter Images, (mr) Ariel Skelley/Corbis, (r) Bruce Hands/Getty Images. Row 2: (l) Digital Stock, (ml) Siede Preis/Getty Images, (mr) Warren Bolster/Getty Images, (r) Pat O'Hara/ Corbis. **117** (tl) S. Nielson/Bruce Coleman. **118** (tl) Dana White/PhotoEdit, (br) Steve Mason/ Getty Images. **119** (tr) NASA Goddard Space Flight Center. **120** (tr) Adastra/Getty Images. **124**, **125**, **126** (all) Liz Garza Williams. **135** (tr) Comstock Images/Alamy. **136** (tr) Radius Images/Alamy. **141** (tl) Deborah Davis/ PhotoEdit, (ml) Tony Freeman/PhotoEdit, (bl) Courtesy of Lawrence Migdale Photography. **142** (tl) Craig Lovell/Corbis, (tr) AFP/Getty Images. **143** (tl) Dean Conger/Corbis, (ml) Getty Images, (mr) Karen Moskowitz/Corbis, (bl) Earl & Nazima Kowall/Corbis, (br) Charles & Josette Lenars/ Corbis. **147** (tl) Ariel Skelly/Corbis, (ml, bl) Getty Images. **149** (tr) Richard Cummins/SuperStock. **150** (tr) Photo Japan/Alamy.

Illustrations

F8, **F9** Liisa Chauncey Guida. **F26** Chi Chung. **2-4**,**14**, **21-22**, **26** Judith DuFour. **31** Norm Bendell. **38-39**, **48** Judith DuFour. **54**, **56-57** Maurie Manning, **64** Norm Bendell. **65** Maurie Manning. **71**, **89**, **110**, **106-108** Judith DuFour. **114** Alex von Dallwitz. **127**, **131-132** Maurie Manning. **133** Norm Bendell. **134**, **140** Judith DuFour. **155-178** Dick Smolinski. **179-182** Lee Woolry. **183-186** Dick Smolinski. **187-190** Den Schofield.

© NGSP & HB